The Time Machine

H. G. Wells

The Time Machine

Text and Study Aids

Edited and annotated by
Werner Sedlak

Ernst Klett Sprachen
Stuttgart

1. Auflage   11 | 2026

Nachfolger von 978-3-12-579801-4
Alle Drucke dieser Auflage sind unverändert und können im Unterricht
nebeneinander verwendet werden.
Die letzte Zahl bezeichnet das Jahr des Druckes. Das Werk und seine
Teile sind urheberrechtlich geschützt. Jede Nutzung in anderen als
den gesetzlich zugelassenen Fällen bedarf der vorherigen schriftlichen
Einwilligung des Verlags.

Edited and annotated by Dr. Werner Sedlak, München

Redaktion: Dr. Hartmut K. Selke
Layoutkonzeption: Elmar Feuerbach
Gestaltung und Satz: bostext, 71292 Friolzheim
Umschlaggestaltung: Sandra Vrabec
Titelbild: Shutterstock (Eugene Ivanov), New York
Foto des Autors: gettyimages (Hulton Archive), München
Druck und Bindung: Digitaldruck Tebben GmbH, Biessenhofen

Printed in Germany
ISBN 978-3-12-579802-1

Contents

Herbert George Wells

About the Author

Herbert George Wells (1866–1946) was born in Bromley, Kent. He was the third son of a shopkeeper, who had been a gardener and cricket professional before marrying a servant. Wells went to Midhurst Grammar School, then was apprenticed to a linen draper when he was 15, but he left in 1883 to become a pupil-teacher at his old school. A year later he began to study biology on a scholarship at the Royal College of Science in London under Thomas Henry Huxley, a leading scientist and humanist who made a deep impression on him. After graduating, he supported himself by teaching and scientific journalism. The publication in 1895 of his first two novels *The Time Machine* and *The Wonderful Visit*, established Wells's literary reputation.

These novels already show two things which characterize all of H. G. Wells's work: his scientific interest in the evolution of the human race and his criticism of the faults of contemporary society.

Besides scientific fantasies like *The Invisible Man* (1897) or *The War of the Worlds* (1898) and Utopian novels like *A Modern Utopia* (1905) and *Men like Gods* (1923), Wells also wrote a great number of short stories, a *Short History of Mankind* (1925), essays and several realistic novels, among which *Tono-Bungay* (1909) and *The History of Mr. Polly* (1910) were the most successful.

Politically, Wells went through various phases. From 1903 to 1908 he was a member of the Fabian Society, a group of moderate Socialists (with the prominent dramatist Bernard Shaw among them) who worked to improve social conditions, especially in London.

During the First World War, Wells was active in the movement which led to the setting up of the League of Nations (a forerunner of the United Nations). Between the Wars he visited many countries, speaking before the Petrograd Soviet, the Reichstag and at the Sorbonne in Paris. In 1934 he had discussions with both Stalin and Roosevelt, trying to interest them in his far-reaching plans for establishing a new peaceful world order. His influence, however, was very limited, and he despaired when the world was involved in war for a second time.

It is as a writer that Wells has been of lasting importance. His *Time Machine*, for example, can be studied as a prototype of science fiction. In this book Wells starts from the scientific concept of a fourth dimension and then leads his readers to imagine a machine that enables its pilot to move freely through time (ch. 1 and 2). The fascinating descriptions of time travelling put everyday human experiences in a different perspective (ch. 3, 11 and 12) by showing, for example, the relativity of the way in which we perceive the flow of time; equally fascinating and also deeply moving is the book's final view of the end of the earth (ch. 11). In the central part of the book, the Time Traveller stops in the world of the year 802,701. The reader's attention is skilfully held as the Time Traveller gradually becomes aware of what threats and horrors are hidden under the surface of a decadent but seemingly peaceful Golden Age (ch. 4 to 10). The final picture of this world can be seen as a pointed criticism of social Darwinism and of its merciless principle of the "survival of the fittest".

Introductory Note

The annotations in this edition explain words not found in the major course books and current word lists. A different standard has been used for the complementary texts in the section *Material for Further Study,* as only such items have been explained that are not found or are difficult to locate in the major monolingual dictionaries currently in use in schools. The following abbreviations are used in this book:

Am. E.	American English	*obs.*	obsolete
apprec.	appreciative	*o.s.*	oneself
B. E.	British English	*pl.*	plural
of.	compare	*poet.*	poetical
ch.	chapter	*sg.*	singular
derog.	derogatory	*sl.*	slang
ed.	editor	*s.o.*	someone
etc.	et cetera, and so on	*s.th.*	something
fig.	figurative	*s.v.*	sub verbo, under the
i.e.	id est, that is		word or heading
lit.	literary	*tech.*	technical
med.	medical		

The Time Machine

1

The Time Traveller (for so it will be convenient to speak of
him) was expounding a recondite matter to us. His grey eyes
shone and twinkled, and his usually pale face was flushed and
5 animated. The fire burned brightly, and the soft radiance of the
incandescent lights in the lilies of silver caught the bubbles that
flashed and passed in our glasses. Our chairs, being his patents,
embraced and caressed us rather than submitted to be sat upon,
and there was that luxurious after-dinner atmosphere when
10 thought runs gracefully free of the trammels of precision. And
he put it to us in this way — marking the points with a lean
forefinger — as we sat and lazily admired his earnestness over
this new paradox (as we thought it) and his fecundity.

"You must follow me carefully. I shall have to controvert one
15 or two ideas that are almost universally accepted. The geometry,
for instance, they taught you at school is founded on a
misconception."

"Is not that rather a large thing to expect us to begin upon?"
said Filby, an argumentative person with red hair.

20 "I do not mean to ask you to accept anything without
reasonable ground for it. You will soon admit as much as I need

---

3 **to expound** to explain – 3 **recondite** [rɪ'kɒndaɪt] difficult to understand – 4 **to
twinkle** *here:* to be bright with excitement and eagerness – 4 **flushed** red because of a
rush of blood to the skin – 5 **animated** full of life – 5 **radiance** warm light –
6 **incandescent** giving out light – 6 **lilies of silver** *here:* candleholders shaped like large
flowers – 7 **patent** ['peɪtnt] – 8 **to embrace** to hold tenderly – 8 **to caress** [kə'res] to
touch in order to show one's love – 8 **to submit** to accept passively – 10 **graceful**
attractive, pleasing – 10 **trammels** restrictions, limits – 11 **to put s.th. to s.o.** to point
out, to explain – 11 **lean** very thin – 12 **forefinger** finger with which one points –
12 **earnestness** seriousness – 13 **paradox** ['pærədɒks] – 13 **fecundity** productiveness –
14 **to controvert** [ˌ--'-] to argue against – 15 **geometry** [dʒɪ'ɒmətrɪ] – 16 **founded on a
misconception** based on a wrong idea – 18 **rather a large thing** *here:* a very general
statement – 19 **argumentative** fond of arguing

from you. You know of course that a mathematical line, a line of thickness *nil,* has no real existence. They taught you that? Neither has a mathematical plane. These things are mere abstractions."

5   "That is all right", said the Psychologist.

"Nor, having only length, breadth, and thickness, can a cube have a real existence."

"There I object," said Filby. "Of course a solid body may exist. All real things —"

10   "So most people think. But wait a moment. Can an *instantaneous* cube exist?"

"Don't follow you," said Filby.

"Can a cube that does not last for any time at all, have a real existence?"

15   Filby became pensive. "Clearly," the Time Traveller proceeded, "any real body must have extension in four directions: it must have Length, Breadth, Thickness, and — Duration. But through a natural infirmity of the flesh, which I will explain to you in a moment, we incline to overlook this fact. There are really four

20 dimensions, three which we call the three planes of Space, and a fourth, Time. There is, however, a tendency to draw an unreal distinction between the former three dimensions and the latter, because it happens that our consciousness moves intermittently in one direction along the latter from the beginning to the end

25 of our lives."

"That," said a very young man, making spasmodic efforts to relight his cigar over the lamp; "that… very clear indeed."

"Now, it is very remarkable that this is so extensively overlooked," continued the Time Traveller, with a slight accession

---

2 **nil** nothing; which cannot be measured – 3 **plane** *here:* flat surface – 6 **cube** solid
body with six equal square sides – 11 **instantaneous** lasting only for a moment –
15 **pensive** deeply thoughtful – 15 **to proceed** to continue – 18 **infirmity of the flesh**
human weakness – 19 **to incline** to have a tendency – 19 **to overlook** not to notice –
21 **to draw a distinction** to make a difference – 22 **the former … the latter** the first …
the last one – 23 **consciousness** what we know and sense in our minds –
23 **intermittently** with interruptions – 26 **spasmodic** repeated, taking place at irregular
intervals – 28 **extensively** widely – 29 **accession** increase

of cheerfulness. "Really this is what is meant by the Fourth Dimension, though some people who talk about the Fourth Dimension do not know they mean it. It is only another way of looking at Time. *There is no difference between Time and any of*
5 *the three dimensions of Space except that our consciousness moves along it.* But some foolish people have got hold of the wrong side of that idea. You have all heard what they have to say about this Fourth Dimension?"

"*I* have not," said the Provincial Mayor.

10 "It is simply this. That Space, as our mathematicians have it, is spoken of as having three dimensions, which one may call Length, Breadth, and Thickness, and is always definable by reference to three planes, each at right angles to the others. But some philosophical people have been asking why *three*
15 dimensions particularly — why not another direction at right angles to the other three? — and have even tried to construct a Four-Dimensional geometry. Professor Simon Newcomb was expounding this to the New York Mathematical Society only a month or so ago. You know how on a flat surface, which has only
20 two dimensions, we can represent a figure of a three-dimensional solid, and similarly they think that by models of three dimensions they could represent one of four — if they could master the perspective of the thing. See?"

"I think so," murmured the Provincial Mayor; and, knitting
25 his brows, he lapsed into an introspective state, his lips moving as one who repeats mystic words. "Yes, I think I see it now," he said after some time, brightening in a quite transitory manner.

---

6 **to get hold of** to understand, to seize – 9 **provincial** *here:* from outside London – 9 **mayor** [mɛə] elected head of a town or city – 10 **have it** tell us, say – 12 **definable by reference to** can be defined by referring to – 17 **Professor Simon Newcomb** (1835–1909), an American astronomer and mathematician – 18 **only a month or so ago** in December 1893 – 24 **to knit one's brows** to show deep thought by frowning – 25 **to lapse into an introspective state** to become deeply absorbed in one's own thoughts – 27 **to brighten** to become more cheerful – 27 **transitory** lasting only for a short time

"Well, I do not mind telling you I have been at work upon this geometry of Four Dimensions for some time. Some of my results are curious. For instance, here is a portrait of a man at eight years old, another at fifteen, another at seventeen, another at
5 twenty-three, and so on. All these are evidently sections, as it were, Three-Dimensional representations of his Four-Dimensioned being, which is a fixed and unalterable thing.

"Scientific people," proceeded the Time Traveller, after the pause required for the proper assimilation of this, "know very
10 well that Time is only a kind of Space. Here is a popular scientific diagram, a weather record. This line I trace with my finger shows the movement of the barometer. Yesterday it was so high, yesterday night it fell, then this morning it rose again, and so gently upward to here. Surely the mercury did not trace this line
15 in any of the dimensions of Space generally recognised? But certainly it traced such a line, and that line, therefore, we must conclude was along the Time-Dimension."

"But," said the Medical Man, staring hard at a coal in the fire, "if Time is really only a fourth dimension of Space, why is it, and
20 why has it always been, regarded as something different? And why cannot we move about in Time as we move about in the other dimensions of Space?"

The Time Traveller smiled. "Are you so sure we can move freely in Space? Right and left we can go, backward and forward freely
25 enough, and men always have done so. I admit we move freely in two dimensions. But how about up and down? Gravitation limits us there."

"Not exactly," said the Medical Man. "There are balloons."

"But before the balloons, save for spasmodic jumping and the
30 inequalities of the surface, man had no freedom of vertical movement."

---

5 **as it were** ... one could say ... – 7 **unalterable** which cannot be changed –
9 **assimilation** understanding – 11 **diagram** ['daɪəgræm] – 14 **mercury** heavy metal (Hg)
used in thermometers and barometers – 14 **to trace** to draw – 29 **save for** except
for – 30 **inequalities** *here:* unevenness of the ground

"Still they could move a little up and down," said the Medical Man.

"Easier, far easier down than up."

"And you cannot move at all in Time, you cannot get away from the present moment."

"My dear sir, that is just where you are wrong. That is just where the whole world has gone wrong. We are always getting away from the present moment. Our mental existences, which are immaterial and have no dimensions, are passing along the Time-Dimension with a uniform velocity from the cradle to the grave. Just as we should travel *down* if we began our existence fifty miles above the earth's surface."

"But the great difficulty is this," interrupted the Psychologist. "You *can* move about in all directions of Space, but you cannot move about in Time."

"That is the germ of my great discovery. But you are wrong to say that we cannot move about in Time. For instance, if I am recalling an incident very vividly I go back to the instant of its occurrence: I become absent-minded, as you say. I jump back for a moment. Of course we have no means of staying back for any length of time, any more than a savage or an animal has of staying six feet above the ground. But a civilised man is better off than the savage in this respect. He can go up against gravitation in a balloon, and why should he not hope that ultimately he may be able to stop or accelerate his drift along the Time-Dimension, or even turn about and travel the other way?"

"Oh, *this*," began Filby, "is all —"

"Why not?" said the Time Traveller.

---

8 **mental existence** the life of the mind – 9 **immaterial** without substance – 10 **uniform** unchanging – 10 **velocity** speed – 10 **cradle** small bed for a baby – 16 **germ** starting-point (of an idea) – 18 **to recall** to remember – 18 **vividly** intensely, clearly – 18 **instant** moment – 19 **of its occurrence** when it happened – 19 **absent-minded** far away in thought – 21 **savage** member of an uncivilized tribe – 25 **ultimately** in the end – 25 **to accelerate** to increase the speed of – 25 **drift** movement, being carried along

"It's against reason," said Filby.

"What reason?" said the Time Traveller.

"You can show black is white by argument," said Filby, "but you will never convince me."

5   "Possibly not," said the Time Traveller. "But now you begin to see the object of my investigations into the geometry of Four Dimensions. Long ago I had a vague inkling of a machine —"

"To travel through Time!" exclaimed the Very Young Man.

"That shall travel indifferently in any direction of Space and
10 Time, as the driver determines."

Filby contented himself with laughter.

"But I have experimental verification," said the Time Traveller.

"It would be remarkably convenient for the historian," the
15 Psychologist suggested. "One might travel back and verify the accepted account of the Battle of Hastings, for instance!"

"Don't you think you would attract attention?" said the Medical Man. "Our ancestors had no great tolerance for anachronisms."

20 "One might get one's Greek from the very lips of Homer and Plato," the Very Young Man thought.

"In which case they would certainly plough you for the Little-go. The German scholars have improved Greek so much."

"Then there is the future," said the Very Young Man. "Just
25 think! One might invest all one's money, leave it to accumulate at interest, and hurry on ahead!"

---

7 **vague** [veɪg] not clear – 7 **inkling** vague idea – 9 **indifferently** *here:* without preference, without noticing any difference – 12 **verification** proof – 15 **to verify** to make sure that s.th. is true – 16 **Battle of Hastings** battle in 1066 in which William the Conqueror defeated the Saxons – 18 **ancestors** one's family further back than one's grandparents – 19 **anachronism** [ə'nækrənɪzm] person or thing that appears to be in the wrong period of time – 20 **from the very lips** directly from the lips – 22 **to plough s.o. for s.th.** *sl.* to make s.o. fail a test – 22 **Little-go** first exam at the University of Cambridge – 23 **scholar** ['skɒlə] person with a great knowledge of a subject – 25 **to accumulate** to increase in quantity – 26 **interest** money paid by a bank on an investment

"To discover a society," said I, "erected on a strictly communistic basis."

"Of all the wild extravagant theories!" began the Psychologist.

5 "Yes, so it seemed to me, and so I never talked of it until —"

"Experimental verification!" cried I. "You are going to verify *that*?"

"The experiment!" cried Filby, who was getting brain-weary.

"Let's see your experiment anyhow," said the Psychologist,
10 "though it's all humbug, you know."

The Time Traveller smiled round at us. Then, still smiling faintly, and with his hands deep in his trousers pockets, he walked slowly out of the room, and we heard his slippers shuffling down the long passage to his laboratory.

15 The Psychologist looked at us. "I wonder what he's got?"

"Some sleight-of-hand trick or other," said the Medical Man, and Filby tried to tell us about a conjurer he had seen at Burslem; but before he had finished his preface the Time Traveller came back, and Filby's anecdote collapsed.

20 The thing the Time Traveller held in his hand was a glittering metallic framework, scarcely larger than a small clock, and very delicately made. There was ivory in it, and some transparent crystalline substance. And now I must be explicit, for this that follows — unless his explanation is to be accepted — is an
25 absolutely unaccountable thing. He took one of the small octagonal tables that were scattered about the room, and set it in front of the fire, with two legs on the hearth rug. On this table he placed the mechanism. Then he drew up a chair, and sat

---

8 **brain-weary** tired of theories and arguments – 14 **to shuffle** to walk slowly without raising the feet properly – 16 **sleight-of-hand trick** [slaɪt] trick done by skilful use of the hands – 17 **conjurer** [kʌndʒərə] man who performs tricks as if by magic – 17 **Burslem** a city in north-west Turkey, also called Bursa – 18 **preface** ['prefəs] introduction to a book, a speech or, here, a story – 21 **framework** structure – 22 **ivory** white bone-like substance – 23 **crystalline** ['krɪstəlaɪn] – 23 **to be explicit** [ɪk'splɪsɪt] to describe or explain in detail – 25 **unaccountable** not to be explained – 26 **octagonal** [ɒk'tægənəl] eight-sided – 27 **hearth rug** carpet in front of the fireplace

down. The only other object on the table was a small shaded lamp, the bright light of which fell full upon the model. There were also perhaps a dozen candles about, two in brass candlesticks upon the mantel and several in sconces, so that
5   the room was brilliantly illuminated. I sat in a low armchair nearest the fire, and I drew this forward so as to be almost between the Time Traveller and the fireplace. Filby sat behind him, looking over his shoulder. The Medical Man and the Provincial Mayor watched him in profile from the right, the
10 Psychologist from the left. The Very Young Man stood behind the Psychologist. We were all on the alert. It appears incredible to me that any kind of trick, however subtly conceived and however adroitly done, could have been played upon us under these conditions.

15   The Time Traveller looked at us, and then at the mechanism. "Well?" said the Psychologist.

     "This little affair," said the Time Traveller, resting his elbows upon the table and pressing his hands together above the apparatus, "is only a model. It is my plan for a machine to travel
20 through time. You will notice that it looks singularly askew, and that there is an odd twinkling appearance about this bar, as though it was in some way unreal." He pointed to the part with his finger. "Also, here is one little white lever, and here is another."

25   The Medical Man got up out of his chair and peered into the thing. "It's beautifully made," he said.

---

1 **shaded** covered by a lamp-shade – 3 **brass** yellow metal made by mixing copper and zinc – 4 **candlestick** holder for a candle – 4 **mantel** shelf on top of a fireplace – 4 **sconce** candleholder fixed to a wall – 5 **brilliantly illuminated** brightly lit – 9 **in profile** ['prəʊfaɪl] from the side – 11 **on the alert** paying close attention – 11 **incredible** unbelievable – 12 **subtle** ['sʌtl] *here:* clever – 13 **adroit** [əˈdrɔɪt] skilful – 19 **apparatus** [ˌæpəˈreɪtəs] mechanism – 20 **singularly** unusually, strangely – 20 **askew** not straight – 21 **odd** strange – 21 **to twinkle** to shine unsteadily – 21 **bar** long piece of metal – 21 **as though** as if – 23 **lever** ['liːvə] bar used to lift or move s.th. – 25 **to peer** to look closely

"It took two years to make," retorted the Time Traveller. Then, when we had all imitated the action of the Medical Man, he said: "Now I want you clearly to understand that this lever, being pressed over, sends the machine gliding into the future, and this
5 other reverses the motion. This saddle represents the seat of a time traveller. Presently I am going to press the lever, and off the machine will go. It will vanish, pass into future Time, and disappear. Have a good look at the thing. Look at the table too, and satisfy yourselves there is no trickery. I don't want to waste
10 this model, and then be told I'm a quack."

There was a minute's pause perhaps. The Psychologist seemed about to speak to me, but changed his mind. Then the Time Traveller put forth his finger towards the lever. "No," he said suddenly. "Lend me your hand." And turning to the Psychologist,
15 he took that individual's hand in his own and told him to put out his forefinger. So that it was the Psychologist himself who sent forth the model Time Machine on its interminable voyage. We all saw the lever turn. I am absolutely certain there was no trickery. There was a breath of wind, and the lamp flame jumped.
20 One of the candles on the mantel was blown out, and the little machine suddenly swung round, became indistinct, was seen as a ghost for a second perhaps, as an eddy of faintly glittering brass and ivory; and it was gone — vanished! Save for the lamp the table was bare.

25 Every one was silent for a minute. Then Filby said he was damned.

The Psychologist recovered from his stupor, and suddenly looked under the table. At that the Time Traveller laughed cheerfully. "Well?" he said, with a reminiscence of the

---

1 **to retort** to give a quick answer – 2 **to imitate** to copy – 4 **to send s.th. gliding** to cause s.th. to move along smoothly – 5 **to reverse** the motion to cause to move in the opposite direction – 7 **to vanish** to become invisible, to disappear – 10 **quack** a person dishonestly claiming to have special knowledge – 17 **interminable** endless – 22 **eddy** circular movement – 22 **to glitter** to shine with flashes of light – 27 **stupor** condition caused by shock or great surprise – 29 **with a reminiscence of** remembering

Psychologist. Then, getting up, he went to the tobacco jar on the mantel, and with his back to us began to fill his pipe.

We stared at each other. "Look here," said the Medical Man, "are you in earnest about this? Do you seriously believe that that
5 machine has travelled into time?"

"Certainly," said the Time Traveller, stooping to light a spill at the fire. Then he turned, lighting his pipe, to look at the Psychologist's face. (The Psychologist, to show that he was not unhinged, helped himself to a cigar and tried to light it uncut.)
10 "What is more, I have a big machine nearly finished in there" — he indicated the laboratory — "and when that is put together I mean to have a journey on my own account."

"You mean to say that that machine has travelled into the future?" said Filby.
15 "Into the future or the past — I don't, for certain, know which."

After an interval the Psychologist had an inspiration. "It must have gone into the past if it has gone anywhere," he said.

"Why?" said the Time Traveller.
20 "Because I presume that it has not moved in space, and if it travelled into the future it would still be here all this time, since it must have travelled through this time."

"But," said I, "if it travelled into the past it would have been visible when we came first into this room; and last Thursday
25 when we were here; and the Thursday before that; and so forth!"

"Serious objections," remarked the Provincial Mayor, with an air of impartiality, turning towards the Time Traveller.

---

1 **jar** container made of glass or stone – 6 **to stoop** to bend down – 6 **spill** thin piece of wood or folded piece of paper for lighting a pipe – 9 **unhinged** off one's balance (of the mind) – 11 **to indicate** to point to – 12 **on my own account** myself – 17 **inspiration** a good idea – 20 **to presume** to suppose – 24 **visible** noticeable to the eye – 28 **impartiality** being fair to both sides

"Not a bit," said the Time Traveller, and, to the Psychologist: "You think. *You* can explain that. It's presentation below the threshold, you know, diluted presentation."

"Of course," said the Psychologist, and reassured us. "That's
5 a simple point of psychology. I should have thought of it. It's plain enough, and helps the paradox delightfully. We cannot see it, nor can we appreciate this machine, any more than we can the spoke of a wheel spinning, or a bullet flying through the air. If it is travelling through time fifty times or a hundred times
10 faster than we are, if it gets through a minute while we get through a second, the impression it creates will of course be only one-fiftieth or one-hundredth of what it would make if it were not travelling in time. That's plain enough." He passed his hand through the space in which the machine had been. "You
15 see?" he said, laughing.

We sat and stared at the vacant table for a minute or so. Then the Time Traveller asked us what we thought of it all.

"It sounds plausible enough tonight," said the Medical Man; "but wait until tomorrow. Wait for the common sense of the
20 morning."

"Would you like to see the Time Machine itself?" asked the Time Traveller. And therewith, taking the lamp in his hand, he led the way down the long, draughty corridor to his laboratory. I remember vividly the flickering light, his queer, broad head in
25 silhouette, the dance of the shadows, how we all followed him, puzzled but incredulous, and how there in the laboratory we beheld a larger edition of the little mechanism which we had

2 **You think**, (stress on 'You') Think about it yourself. – 2 **below the threshold** below the level at which it can be seen – 3 **diluted presentation** presentation to the eye is weakened – 4 **to reassure** to remove s.o.'s doubts – 7 **to appreciate** *here:* to see, to understand fully – 8 **spoke** any one of the bars connecting the centre of a wheel with the outer edge – 8 **to spin** to go round and round very fast – 16 **vacant** empty – 18 **plausible** ['plɔːzəbl] convincing – 22 **therewith** *formal:* with this, then – 23 **draughty** ['drɑːftɪ] with cold air blowing through – 24 **to flicker** to shine unsteadily – 24 **queer** unusual – 25 **silhouette** [ˌsɪluːet] – 26 **puzzled** perplexed, confused – 26 **incredulous** unbelieving – 27 **to behold, beheld, beheld** *lit.* to see – 27 **edition** *here:* version

seen vanish from before our eyes. Parts were of nickel, parts of ivory, parts had certainly been filed or sawn out of rock crystal. The thing was generally complete, but the twisted crystalline bars lay unfinished upon the bench beside some sheets of
5 drawings, and I took one up for a better look at it. Quartz it seemed to be.

"Look here," said the Medical Man, "are you perfectly serious? Or is this a trick — like that ghost you showed us last Christmas?"

10 "Upon that machine," said the Time Traveller, holding the lamp aloft, "I intend to explore time. Is that plain? I was never more serious in my life."

None of us quite knew how to take it.

I caught Filby's eye over the shoulder of the Medical Man, and
15 he winked at me solemnly.

2

I think that at that time none of us quite believed in the Time Machine. The fact is, the Time Traveller was one of those men who are too clever to be believed: you never felt that you saw
20 all round him; you always suspected some subtle reserve, some ingenuity in ambush, behind his lucid frankness. Had Filby shown the model and explained the matter in the Time Traveller's words, we should have shown *him* far less scepticism. For we should have perceived his motives: a pork butcher could
25 understand Filby. But the Time Traveller had more than a touch

2 **to file** to shape with a file – 4 **bench** table for working and sawing on – 11 **aloft** up high – 13 **how to take it** *here:* what to think of it – 15 **to wink** to close and open an eye rapidly, here as a sign of amusement – 20 **to suspect s.th.** to have a feeling about the existence of s.th. – 20 **reserve** *here:* an unexpected idea ready for use if needed – 21 **ingenuity** cleverness – 21 **in ambush** hidden and ready for a surprise attack – 21 **lucid** easy to understand – 21 **frankness** honesty, openness – 23 **scepticism** ['skeptɪsɪzəm] doubt – 24 **to perceive** to see, to understand – 25 **a touch of** a small quantity of

of whim among his elements, and we distrusted him. Things that would have made the fame of a less clever man seemed tricks in his hands. It is a mistake to do things too easily. The serious people who took him seriously never felt quite sure of his deportment: they were somehow aware that trusting their reputations for judgment with him was like furnishing a nursery with egg-shell china. So I don't think any of us said very much about time travelling in the interval between that Thursday and the next, though its odd potentialities ran, no doubt, in most of our minds: its plausibility, that is, its practical incredibleness, the curious possibilities of anachronism and of utter confusion it suggested. For my own part, I was particularly preoccupied with the trick of the model. That I remember discussing with the Medical Man, whom I met on Friday at the Linnaean. He said he had seen a similar thing at Tubingen, and laid considerable stress on the blowing out of the candle. But how the trick was done he could not explain.

The next Thursday I went again to Richmond — I suppose I was one of the Time Traveller's most constant guests — and, arriving late, found four or five men already assembled in his drawing-room. The Medical Man was standing before the fire with a sheet of paper in one hand and his watch in the other. I looked round for the Time Traveller, and — "It's half past seven now," said the Medical Man. "I suppose we'd better have dinner?"

---

1 **whim** a sudden idea, often unusual or unreasonable – 1 **element** *here:* part of a person's character or temperament – 1 **to distrust** to have no confidence in – 2 **to make the fame of s.o.** to make s.o. famous – 5 **deportment** behaviour – 5 **to trust s.th. with s.o.** to put s.th. in s.o.'s hands to be used or looked after – 6 **reputation for judgement** general opinion that one is able to judge people and situations correctly – 6 **nursery** room for a baby or young children – 7 **egg-shell china** thin and valuable porcelain – 9 **potentialities** possibilities – 10 **incredibleness** lack of probability – 11 **utter** total, complete – 12 **to be preoccupied with** to give one's attention completely to s.th. – 13 **That I remember** … I remember discussing that trick – 14 **the Linnaean** the Linnaean Society (for natural history) – 18 **Richmond** suburb in the west of London where upper- and middle-class people have their homes – 20 **to assemble** to come together – 21 **drawing-room** room where guests are received

"Where's —?" said I, naming our host.

"You've just come? It's rather odd. He's unavoidably detained. He asks me in this note to lead off with dinner at seven if he's not back. Says he'll explain when he comes."

5 "It seems a pity to let the dinner spoil," said the Editor of a well-known daily paper; and thereupon the Doctor rang the bell.

The Psychologist was the only person besides the Doctor and myself who had attended the previous dinner. The other men 10 were Blank, the Editor aforementioned, a certain journalist, and another — a quiet, shy man with a beard — whom I didn't know, and who, as far as my observation went, never opened his mouth all the evening. There was some speculation at the dinner table about the Time Traveller's absence, and I suggested time 15 travelling, in a half jocular spirit. The Editor wanted that explained to him, and the Psychologist volunteered a wooden account of the "ingenious paradox and trick" we had witnessed that day week. He was in the midst of his exposition when the door from the corridor opened slowly and without noise. I was 20 facing the door, and saw it first. "Hallo!" I said. "At last!" And the door opened wider, and the Time Traveller stood before us. I gave a cry of surprise. "Good heavens! man, what's the matter?" cried the Medical Man, who saw him next. And the whole tableful turned towards the door.

25 He was in an amazing plight. His coat was dusty and dirty, and smeared with green down the sleeves; his hair disordered, and as it seemed to me greyer — either with dust and dirt or because its colour had actually faded. His face was ghastly pale; his chin had a brown cut on it — a cut half healed; his expression

---

2 **detained** prevented from arriving on time – 3 **to lead off** to begin – 5 **editor** person who plans and directs the publication of a paper, magazine or book – 6 **thereupon** *formal* then – 9 **previous** the one before – 10 **aforementioned** *dated:* named before – 15 **jocular** not serious, joking – 16 **to volunteer** to offer – 17 **ingenious** very clever – 18 **that day week** on the same day a week before – 18 **exposition** account, explanation – 25 **plight** serious state – 26 **smeared with** covered with s.th. oily or sticky – 28 **ghastly** very pale and ill-looking

was haggard and drawn, as by intense suffering. For a moment he hesitated in the doorway, as if he had been dazzled by the light. Then he came into the room. He walked with just such a limp as I have seen in footsore tramps. We stared at him in silence, expecting him to speak.

He said not a word, but came painfully to the table, and made a motion towards the wine. The Editor filled a glass of champagne, and pushed it towards him. He drained it, and it seemed to do him good: for he looked round the table, and the ghost of his old smile flickered across his face. "What on earth have you been up to, man?" said the Doctor. The Time Traveller did not seem to hear. "Don't let me disturb you " he said, with a certain faltering articulation. "I'm all right." He stopped, held out his glass for more, and took it off at a draught. "That's good," he said. His eyes grew brighter, and a faint colour came into his cheeks. His glance flickered over our faces with a certain dull approval, and then went round the warm and comfortable room. Then he spoke again, still as it were feeling his way among his words. "I'm going to wash and dress, and then I'll come down and explain things. … Save me some of that mutton. I'm starving for a bit of meat."

He looked across at the Editor, who was a rare visitor, and hoped he was all right. The Editor began a question. "Tell you presently," said the Time Traveller. "I'm — funny! Be all right in a minute."

He put down his glass, and walked towards the staircase door. Again I remarked his lameness and the soft padding sound of his football, and standing up in my place, I saw his feet as he

---

1 **haggard** looking extremely tired and lined – 1 **drawn** *here:* pulled out of shape with pain and tiredness – 2 **dazzled** made unable to see clearly because of too much light – 4 **limp** lame and uneven walk – 8 **to drain** *here:* to empty – 10 **What have you been up to?** What have you been doing? – 12 **faltering** hesitating, unsteady – 14 **to take it off at a draught** to empty it (a glass) all at once – 16 **dull** *here:* inexpressive – 20 **mutton** meat from a sheep – 20 **to starve for s.th.** to long for s.th. desperately – 24 **presently** in a minute – 26 **staircase door** door leading to the stairs – 27 **to pad** to walk making a soft sound

went out. He had nothing on them but a pair of tattered, bloodstained socks. Then the door closed upon him. I had half a mind to follow, till I remembered how he detested any fuss about himself. For a minute, perhaps, my mind was wool
5 gathering. Then, "Remarkable Behaviour of an Eminent Scientist." I heard the Editor say, thinking (after his wont) in headlines. And this brought my attention back to the bright dinner table.

"What's the game?" said the Journalist. "Has he been doing
10 the Amateur Cadger? I don't follow."I met the eye of the Psychologist, and read my own interpretation in his face. I thought of the Time Traveller limping painfully upstairs. I don't think any one else had noticed his lameness.

The first to recover completely from this surprise was the
15 Medical Man, who rang the bell — the Time Traveller hated to have servants waiting at dinner — for a hot plate. At that the Editor turned to his knife and fork with a grunt, and the Silent Man followed suit. The dinner was resumed. Conversation was exclamatory for a little while, with gaps of wonderment; and
20 then the Editor got fervent in his curiosity. "Does our friend eke out his modest income with a crossing? or has he his Nebuchadnezzar phases?" he inquired. "I feel assured it's this business of the Time Machine," I said, and took up the Psychologist's account of our previous meeting. The new guests
25 were frankly incredulous. The Editor raised objections. "What

---

1 **tattered** torn – 2 **I had half a mind to** I almost decided to – 3 **to detest** to hate – 4 **wool gathering** not concentrated – 5 **eminent** famous, leading – 6 **after his wont** [wəʊnt] *dated:* as was his habit – 9 **What's the game?** What's he playing at? – 9 **to do the Amateur Cadger** to act a beggar for enjoyment – 16 **at that** after which – 17 **grunt** low, rough sound expressing irritation – 18 **to follow suit** to do the same – 18 **to resume** to continue – 19 **exclamatory** consisting of exclamations – 19 **wonderment** surprise – 20 **fervent** very eager – 20 **to eke out his modest income** to earn a small amount of money with great difficulty – 21 **with a crossing** *probably* by sweeping a street crossing – 22 **Nebuchadnezzar phase** [ˌnɛbjʊkedˈnezə] period of madness during which s.o. lives outside human society and eats grass like an animal (cf. the Old Testament, Daniel Ch. 4)

was this time travelling? A man couldn't cover himself with dust by rolling in a paradox, could he?" And then, as the idea came home to him, he resorted to caricature. Hadn't they any clothes-brushes in the Future? The Journalist, too, would not believe at
5 any price, and joined the Editor in the easy work of heaping ridicule on the whole thing. They were both the new kind of journalist — very joyous, irreverent young men. "Our Special Correspondent in the Day after Tomorrow reports," the Journalist was saying — or rather shouting — when the Time Traveller
10 came back. He was dressed in ordinary evening clothes, and nothing save his haggard look remained of the change that had startled me.

"I say," said the Editor hilariously, "these chaps here say you have been travelling into the middle of next week!! Tell us all
15 about little Rosebery, will you? What will you take for the lot?"

The Time Traveller came to the place reserved for him without a word. He smiled quietly, in his old way. "Where's my mutton?" he said. "What a treat it is to stick a fork into meat again!"

"Story!" cried the Editor.

20 "Story be damned!" said the Time Traveller. "I want something to eat. I won't say a word until I get some peptone into my arteries. Thanks. And the salt."

"One word," said I. "Have you been time travelling?"

"Yes," said the Time Traveller, with his mouth full, nodding
25 his head.

"I'd give a shilling a line for a verbatim note," said the Editor.

The Time Traveller pushed his glass towards the Silent Man and

---

2 **an idea comes home to s.o.** s.o. becomes fully conscious of an idea – 3 **to resort to** to turn to s.th. for help – 5 **to heap ridicule on** to make fun of – 7 **joyous** merry – 7 **irreverent** lacking respect – 13 **hilarious** laughing loudly – 13 **chap** fellow – 15 **Lord Rosebery** British Prime Minister from 3rd March 1894 to 21st June 1895; he was very popular ("little R.") as the owner of successful race-horses ("the middle of next week" probably refers to coming horse-races). – 15 **What will you take for the lot?** How much money do you want for the whole story? – 18 **treat** pleasure – 21 **peptone** substance coming from proteins – 26 **shilling** (until 1971) a coin worth one twentieth of a pound – 26 **verbatim note** a word-for-word report (of the Time Traveller's story)

rang it with his finger nail; at which the Silent Man, who had been staring at his face, started convulsively, and poured him wine. The rest of the dinner was uncomfortable. For my own part, sudden questions kept on rising to my lips, and I dare say it was the same with the others. The Journalist tried to relieve the tension by telling anecdotes of Hettie Potter. The Time Traveller devoted his attention to his dinner, and displayed the appetite of a tramp. The Medical Man smoked a cigarette, and watched the Time Traveller through his eyelashes. The Silent Man seemed even more clumsy than usual, and drank champagne with regularity and determination out of sheer nervousness. At last the Time Traveller pushed his plate away, and looked round us. "I suppose I must apologise," he said. "I was simply starving. I've had a most amazing time." He reached out his hand for a cigar, and cut the end. "But come into the smoking-room. It's too long a story to tell over greasy plates." And ringing the bell in passing, he led the way into the adjoining room.

"You have told Blank, and Dash, and Chose about the machine?" he said to me, leaning back in his easy chair and naming the three new guests.

"But the thing's a mere paradox," said the Editor.

"I can't argue tonight. I don't mind telling you the story, but I can't argue. I will," he went on, "tell you the story of what has happened to me, if you like, but you must refrain from interruptions. I want to tell it. Badly. Most of it will sound like lying. So be it! It's true — every word of it, all the same. I was in my laboratory at four o'clock, and since then … I've lived eight

---

2 **to start** *here:* to make a sudden movement from surprise – 2 **convulsive** violent – 5 **to relieve** to reduce – 6 **tension** nervousness and excitement – 6 **Hettie Potter** probably a well-known personality of the 1890s – 7 **to devote one's attention to** to give one's full attention to – 7 **to display** to show – 9 **eyelashes** hairs on the edge of the eyelid – 11 **sheer** pure – 13 **to apologise** to say one is sorry – 16 **greasy** covered with fat – 17 **adjoining** next – 20 **easy chair** big soft chair with arms – 22 **mere** nothing but – 25 **to refrain from** to hold oneself back – 26 **badly** *here:* very much

days … such days as no human being ever lived before! I'm nearly worn out, but I shan't sleep till I've told this thing over to you. Then I shall go to bed. But no interruptions! Is it agreed?"

"Agreed," said the Editor, and the rest of us echoed "Agreed."
And with that the Time Traveller began his story as I have set it forth. He sat back in his chair at first, and spoke like a weary man. Afterwards he got more animated. In writing it down I feel with only too much keenness the inadequacy of pen and ink — and, above all, my own inadequacy — to express its quality. You read, I will suppose, attentively enough; but you cannot see the speaker's white, sincere face in the bright circle of the little lamp, nor hear the intonation of his voice. You cannot know how his expression followed the turns of his story! Most of us hearers were in shadow, for the candles in the smoking-room had not been lighted, and only the face of the Journalist and the legs of the Silent Man from the knees downward were illuminated. At first we glanced now and again at each other. After a time we ceased to do that, and looked only at the Time Traveller's face.

3

"I told some of you last Thursday of the principles of the Time Machine, and showed you the actual thing itself, incomplete in the workshop. There it is now, a little travel-worn, truly; and one of the ivory bars is cracked, and a brass rail bent; but the rest of it's sound enough. I expected to finish it on Friday; but on Friday, when the putting together was nearly done, I found that one of the nickel bars was exactly one inch too short, and this I had to get remade; so that the thing was not complete until this morning. It was at ten o'clock today that the first of all Time

---

5 **to set s.th. forth** to present s.th. – 8 **with only too much keenness** *here:* only too strongly – 9 **inadequacy** insufficient possibilities – 25 **sound** *here:* in good condition – 27 **inch** = 2.5 centimetres – 28 **to get s.th. remade** to have s.th. made again

Machines began its career. I gave it a last tap, tried all the screws again, put one more drop of oil on the quartz rod, and sat myself in the saddle. I suppose a suicide who holds a pistol to his skull feels much the same wonder at what will come next as I felt
5 then. I took the starting lever in one hand and the stopping one in the other, pressed the first, and almost immediately the second. I seemed to reel; I felt a nightmare sensation of falling; and, looking round, I saw the laboratory exactly as before. Had anything happened? For a moment I suspected that my intellect
10 had tricked me. Then I noted the clock. A moment before, as it seemed, it had stood at a minute or so past ten; now it was nearly half past three!

"I drew a breath, set my teeth, gripped the starting lever with both hands, and went off with a thud. The laboratory got hazy
15 and went dark. Mrs. Watchett came in and walked, apparently without seeing me, towards the garden door. I suppose it took her a minute or so to traverse the place, but to me she seemed to shoot across the room like a rocket. I pressed the lever over to its extreme position. The night came like the turning out of
20 a lamp, and in another moment came tomorrow. The laboratory grew faint and hazy, then fainter and ever fainter. Tomorrow night came black, then day again, night again, day again, faster and faster still. An eddying murmur filled my ears, and a strange, dumb confusedness descended on my mind.

25 "I am afraid I cannot convey the peculiar sensations of time travelling. They are excessively unpleasant. There is a feeling exactly like that one has upon a switchback — of a helpless

---

3 **a suicide** *here:* a person who is about to commit suicide – 7 **to reel** to stand or move unsteadily – 7 **sensation** *here:* feeling – 9 **intellect** mind – 13 **to set one's teeth** to hold one's teeth together firmly and become determined – 13 **to grip** to take hold of firmly – 14 **thud** dull sound - hazy unclear, misty – 15 **Mrs. Watchett** a servant – 17 **to traverse** to pass through – 24 **dumb** making it impossible to express oneself, silent – 24 **to descend on** to come down on – 25 **to convey** to express, to communicate – 26 **excessively** extremely – 27 **switchback** railways with steep ups and downs, especially the kind seen in amusement parks

headlong motion! I felt the same horrible anticipation, too, of an imminent smash. As I put on pace, night followed day like the flapping of a black wing. The dim suggestion of the laboratory seemed presently to fall away from me, and saw the sun hopping
5 swiftly across the sky, leaping it every minute, and every minute marking a day. I supposed the laboratory had been destroyed and I had come into the open air. I had a dim impression of scaffolding, but I was already going too fast to be conscious of any moving things. The slowest snail that ever crawled dashed
10 by too fast for me. The twinkling succession of darkness and light was excessively painful to the eye. Then, in the intermittent darknesses, I saw the moon spinning swiftly through her quarters from new to full, and had a faint glimpse of the circling stars. Presently, as I went on, still gaining velocity, the palpitation of
15 night and day merged into one continuous greyness; the sky took on a wonderful deepness of blue, a splendid luminous colour like that of early twilight; the jerking sun became a streak of fire, a brilliant arch, in space; the moon a fainter fluctuating band; and I could see nothing of the stars, save now and then
20 a brighter circle flickering in the blue.

"The landscape was misty and vague. I was still on the hillside upon which this house now stands, and the shoulder rose above me grey and dim. I saw trees growing and changing like puffs of vapour, now brown, now green; they grew, spread, shivered,
25 and passed away. I saw huge buildings rise up faint and fair, and

---

1 **headlong** head first and at great speed – 1 **anticipation** expectation – 2 **to put on pace** to move faster and faster, to accelerate – 3 **flapping** slow movement up and down – 3 **dim** unclear, vague – 4 **to hop** to jump – 5 **swiftly** rapidly, fast – 5 **to leap s.th.** to jump across s.th. – 8 **scaffolding** wooden structure, usually put up in order to repair a house – 9 **snail** small soft animal with a shell; it moves very slowly – 9 **to crawl** to creep, to move very slowly – 9 **to dash by** to pass by very rapidly – 13 **glimpse** short and incomplete view – 14 **palpitation** rapid rhythm – 15 **to merge into** to become one with, to change gradually into – 16 **luminous** shining, bright – 17 **twilight** half-light before sunrise or after sunset – 17 **streak** thin line – 18 **arch** curved shape or structure – 18 **to fluctuate** to rise and fall – 22 **shoulder** *here:* of the hill – 23 **puff of vapour** sudden short sending out of steam – 24 **to shiver** to shake, tremble

pass like dreams. The whole surface of the earth seemed changed — melting and flowing under my eyes. The little hands upon the dials that registered my speed raced round faster and faster. Presently I noted that the sun belt swayed up and down, from
5 solstice to solstice, in a minute or less, and that consequently my pace was over a year a minute; and minute by minute the white snow flashed across the world, and vanished, and was followed by the bright, brief green of spring.

"The unpleasant sensations of the start were less poignant
10 now. They merged at last into a kind of hysterical exhilaration. I remarked indeed a clumsy swaying of the machine, for which I was unable to account. But my mind was too confused to attend to it, so with a kind of madness growing upon me, I flung myself into futurity. At first I scarce thought of stopping, scarce
15 thought of anything but these new sensations. But presently a fresh series of impressions grew up in my mind — a certain curiosity and therewith a certain dread — until at last they took complete possession of me. What strange developments of humanity, what wonderful advances upon our rudimentary
20 civilisation, I thought, might not appear when I came to look nearly into the dim elusive world that raced and fluctuated before my eyes! I saw great and splendid architecture rising about me, more massive than any buildings of our own time, and yet, as it seemed, built of glimmer and mist. I saw a richer
25 green flow up the hillside, and remain there without any wintry intermission. Even through the veil of my confusion the earth seemed very fair. And so my mind came round to the business of stopping.

---

3 **dial** the front of a clock-like instrument – 4 **belt** band, streak – 4 **to sway** to swing, to move – 5 **solstice** ['sɒlstɪs] time at which the sun is farthest north or south of the equator – 5 **consequently** therefore – 6 **pace** speed – 8 **brief** short – 9 **poignant** sharp, violent – 10 **exhilaration** excitement, high spirits – 12 **to account for s.th.** to explain s. th. – 13 **to fling, flung, flung** to throw with force – 14 **futurity** future time – 17 **dread** anxiety, fear – 19 **advances** *here:* improvements – 19 **rudimentary** simple, undeveloped – 21 **elusive** moving fast, therefore difficult to see clearly – 24 **glimmer** faint, unsteady light – 26 **intermission** pause, interruption – 27 **to come round to** *here:* finally to pay attention to

"The peculiar risk lay in the possibility of my finding some substance in the space which I, or the machine, occupied. So long as I travelled at a high velocity through time, this scarcely mattered; I was, so to speak, attenuated — was slipping like a vapour through the interstices of intervening substances! But to come to a stop involved the jamming of myself, molecule by molecule, into whatever lay in my way; meant bringing my atoms into such intimate contact with those of the obstacle that a profound chemical reaction — possibly a far-reaching explosion — would result, and blow myself and my apparatus out of all possible dimensions — into the Unknown. This possibility had occurred to me again and again while I was making the machine; but then I had cheerfully accepted it as an unavoidable risk — one of the risks a man has got to take! Now the risk was inevitable, I no longer saw it in the same cheerful light. The fact is that, insensibly, the absolute strangeness of everything, the sickly jarring and swaying of the machine, above all, the feeling of prolonged falling, had absolutely upset my nerve. I told myself that I could never stop, and with a gust of petulance I resolved to stop forthwith. Like an impatient fool, I lugged over the lever, and incontinently the thing went reeling over, and I was flung headlong through the air.

"There was the sound of a clap of thunder in my ears. I may have been stunned for a moment. A pitiless hail was hissing round me, and I was sitting on soft turf in front of the overset

4 **attenuated** diluted, made thinner – 5 **interstice** [ɪnˈtɜːstɪs] very small crack or space in s.th. – 5 **to intervene** [ˌɪntəˈviːn] to come or be between – 6 **to jam** to press, to crush – 8 **intimate** [ˈ---] close – 8 **obstacle** s.th. which stands in the way – 16 **insensibly** *here:* gradually, without being noticed – 16 **sickly** causing a sick feeling – 17 **jarring** harsh sound or vibration – 18 **to upset** to disturb – 19 **gust** sudden outburst – 19 **petulance** bad temper, impatience – 19 **to resolve** to decide – 20 **forthwith** *lit.* at once – 20 **to lug** to pull with great effort – 21 **incontinently** *obs.* without delay, at once – 21 **to go reeling over** *here:* to roll or fall over – 23 **clap** loud explosive sound – 24 **to stun** to make unconscious, to confuse the mind – 24 **hail** frozen raindrops – 24 **to hiss** to make the sound of water falling on a very hot surface – 25 **turf** grass-covered earth – 25 **overset** thrown over, overturned

machine. Everything still seemed grey, but presently I remarked that the confusion in my ears was gone. I looked round me. I was on what seemed to be a little lawn in a garden, surrounded by rhododendron bushes, and I noticed that their mauve and
5 purple blossoms were dropping in a shower under the beating of the hailstones. The rebounding, dancing hail hung in a cloud over the machine, and drove along the ground like smoke. In a moment I was wet to the skin. 'Fine hospitality,' said I, 'to a man who has travelled innumerable years to see you.'

10 "Presently I thought what a fool I was to get wet. I stood up and looked round me. A colossal figure, carved apparently in some white stone, loomed indistinctly beyond the rhododendrons through the hazy downpour. But all else of the world was invisible.

15 "My sensations would be hard to describe. As the columns of hail grew thinner, I saw the white figure more distinctly. It was very large, for a silver birch-tree touched its shoulder. It was of white marble, in shape something like a winged sphinx, but the wings, instead of being carried vertically at the sides, were spread
20 so that it seemed to hover. The pedestal, it appeared to me, was of bronze, and was thick with verdigris. It chanced that the face was towards me; the sightless eyes seemed to watch me; there was the faint shadow of a smile on the lips. It was greatly weather-worn, and that imparted an unpleasant suggestion of disease.
25 I stood looking at it for a little space — half a minute, perhaps, or half an hour. It seemed to advance and to recede as the hail drove before it denser or thinner. At last I tore my eyes from it

---

4 **mauve** bright, pale purple – 5 **blossom** flower on a bush or tree – 6 **to rebound** to spring back after hitting s.th. – 8 **hospitality** welcome – 9 **innumerable** too many to be counted – 11 **colossal** [-'--] – 11 **to carve** *here:* to cut – 11 **apparently** it would seem – 12 **to loom indistinctly** to appear but without a clear form – 13 **downpour** heavy rain – 17 **birch-tree** tree with white bark which grows in northern countries – 18 **marble** hard stone used for buildings and sculptures – 20 **to hover** to remain in the air at one place – 20 **pedestal** ['---] base of a statue or column – 21 **verdigris** ['ʌɜ:dɪɡrɪs] green substance which forms on brass and bronze surfaces – 21 **to chance** to happen – 24 **to impart** to give, to lend – 26 **to recede** to move back or away

for a moment, and saw that the hail curtain had worn threadbare, and that the sky was lightening with the promise of the sun.

"I looked up again at the crouching white shape, and the full temerity of my voyage came suddenly upon me. What might
5 appear when that hazy curtain was altogether withdrawn? What might not have happened to men? What if cruelty had grown into a common passion? What if in this interval the race had lost its manliness, and had developed into something inhuman, unsympathetic, and overwhelmingly powerful? I might seem some
10 old-world savage animal, only the more dreadful and disgusting for our common likeness — a foul creature to be incontinently slain.

"Already I saw other vast shapes — huge buildings with intricate
15 parapets and tall columns, with a wooded hillside dimly creeping in upon me through the lessening storm. I was seized with a panic fear. I turned frantically to the Time Machine, and strove hard to readjust it. As I did so the shafts of the sun smote through the thunderstorm. The grey downpour was swept aside and
20 vanished like the trailing garments of a ghost. Above me, in the intense blue of the summer sky, some faint brown shreds of cloud whirled into nothingness. The great buildings about me stood out clear and distinct, shining with the wet of the thunderstorm, and picked out in white by the unmelted
25 hailstones piled along their courses. I felt naked in a strange

---

1 **to wear threadbare** to become thin and transparent – 3 **to crouch** to lower the body with the arms and legs held in close – 4 **temerity** foolish boldness – 5 **to withdraw** *here:* to draw or take away – 7 **race** *here:* human race – 8 **manliness** qualities expected of a man – 9 **unsympathetic** without pity – 9 **overwhelming** extreme – 11 **savage** not tame, wild – 11 **disgusting** very unpleasant – 12 **likeness** similar form – 12 **a foul creature** a very ugly being – 13 **to slay, slew, slain** *lit.* to kill – 14 **intricate** ['---] complicated – 15 **parapet** low wall at the side of roof, bridge, etc. – 17 **frantically** wildly excited because of fear – 17 **to strive, strove, striven** to struggle hard – 18 **to readjust** to put back into its proper position – 18 **shaft** ray of light – 18 **to smite, smote, smitten** *lit.* to strike – 20 **to trail** *here:* to be dragged along behind – 20 **garments** clothes – 21 **shreds** pieces torn off s.th. – 22 **to whirl** to move quickly round and round – 24 **picked out** standing out clearly – 25 **naked** ['neɪkɪd] without clothes on

world. I felt as perhaps a bird may feel in the clear air, knowing the hawk wings above and will swoop. My fear grew to frenzy. I took a breathing space, set my teeth, and again grappled fiercely, wrist and knee, with the machine. It gave under my desperate onset and turned over. It struck my chin violently. One hand on the saddle, the other on the lever, I stood panting heavily in attitude to mount again.

"But with this recovery of a prompt retreat my courage recovered. I looked more curiously and less fearfully at this world of the remote future. In a circular opening, high up in the wall of the nearer house, I saw a group of figures clad in rich soft robes. They had seen me, and their faces were directed towards me.

"Then I heard voices approaching me. Coming through the bushes by the White Sphinx were the heads and shoulders of men running. One of these emerged in a pathway leading straight to the little lawn upon which I stood with my machine. He was a slight creature — perhaps four feet high — clad in a purple tunic, girdled at the waist with a leather belt. Sandals or buskins — I could not clearly distinguish which — were on his feet; his legs were bare to the knees, and his head was bare. Noticing that, I noticed for the first time how warm the air was.

"He struck me as being a very beautiful and graceful creature, but indescribably frail. His flushed face reminded me of the more beautiful kind of consumptive — that hectic beauty of which we used to hear so much. At the sight of him I suddenly regained confidence. I took my hands from the machine.

---

2 **hawk** strong, fast bird which lives off small animals – 2 **to swoop** to rush down suddenly – 2 **frenzy** an attack (as if) of madness – 3 **to grapple with** to struggle with – 3 **fiercely** violently – 4 **It gave** *here:* It moved – 5 **onset** attack – 6 **to pant** to breathe quickly after an effort – 6 **in attitude** *here:* ready and intending – 7 **to mount** to climb into the saddle – 8 **recovery** regaining of s.th. lost – 8 **retreat** a way of escaping – 10 **remote** far – 11 **clad** *lit.* dressed – 15 **to emerge** to appear – 17 **slight** small and weak-looking – 18 **tunic** loose piece of outer clothing reaching to the knees – 18 **girdled** with a belt round – 19 **buskins** half boots – 20 **bare** uncovered – 23 **to strike as** to give the impression of – 24 **frail** weak, slight in body – 25 **consumptive** person who suffers from tuberculosis – 25 **hectic** unnaturally red, feverish – 27 **to regain** to win back

4

"In another moment we were standing face to face, I and this fragile thing out of futurity. He came straight up to me and laughed into my eyes. The absence from his bearing of any sign of fear struck me at once. Then he turned to the two others who were following him and spoke to them in a strange and very sweet and liquid tongue.

"There were others coming, and presently a little group of perhaps eight or ten of these exquisite creatures were about me. One of them addressed me. It came into my head, oddly enough, that my voice was too harsh and deep for them. So I shook my head, and, pointing to my ears, shook it again. He came a step forward, hesitated, and then touched my hand. Then I felt other soft little tentacles upon my back and shoulders. They wanted to make sure I was real. There was nothing in this at all alarming. Indeed, there was something in these pretty little people that inspired confidence — a graceful gentleness, a certain childlike ease. And besides, they looked so frail that I could fancy myself flinging the whole dozen of them about like nine-pins. But I made a sudden motion to warn them when I saw their little pink hands feeling at the Time Machine. Happily then, when it was not too late, I thought of a danger I had hitherto forgotten, and reaching over the bars of the machine I unscrewed the little levers that would set it in motion, and put these in my pocket. Then I turned again to see what I could do in the way of communication.

"And then, looking more nearly into their features, I saw some further peculiarities in their Dresden-china type of prettiness. Their hair, which was uniformly curly, came to a sharp end at

---

3 **fragile** ['frædʒaɪl] frail – 4 **bearing** way of behaving – 7 **liquid** *here:* clear and flowing – 11 **harsh** *here:* unpleasant to the ears – 14 **tentacles** long boneless 'arms' for feeling – 19 **nine-pins** game in which bottle-shaped pieces of wood are knocked down by a ball – 22 **hitherto** *formal:* up to that moment – 27 **features** face or parts of the face – 28 **Dresden-china type** like porcelain from Meissen – 29 **curly** shaped like a spiral

the neck and cheek; there was not the faintest suggestion of it on the face, and their ears were singularly minute. The mouths were small, with bright red, rather thin lips, and the little chins ran to a point. The eyes were large and mild; and — this may
5 seem egotism on my part — I fancied even then that there was a certain lack of the interest I might have expected in them.

"As they made no effort to communicate with me, but simply stood round me smiling and speaking in soft cooing notes to each other, I began the conversation. I pointed to the Time
10 Machine and to myself. Then, hesitating for a moment how to express time, I pointed to the sun. At once a quaintly pretty little figure in chequered purple and white followed my gesture, and then astonished me by imitating the sound of thunder.

"For a moment I was staggered, though the import of his
15 gesture was plain enough. The question had come into my mind abruptly: were these creatures fools? You may hardly understand how it took me. You see I had always anticipated that the people of the year Eight Hundred and Two Thousand odd would be incredibly in front of us in knowledge, art, everything. Then one
20 of them suddenly asked me a question that showed him to be on the intellectual level of one of our five-year-old children — asked me, in fact, if I had come from the sun in a thunderstorm! It let loose the judgment I had suspended upon their clothes, their frail light limbs, and fragile features. A flow of
25 disappointment rushed across my mind. For a moment I felt that I had built the Time Machine in vain.

"I nodded, pointed to the sun, and gave them such a vivid rendering of a thunderclap as startled them. They all withdrew a pace or so and bowed. Then came one laughing towards me,

2 **minute** [maɪˈnjuːt] very small – 5 **egotism** self-centredness, self-importance – 5 **to fancy** to be under the impression – 8 **to coo** to make a soft, murmuring sound (like a pigeon) – 11 **quaint** unusual and attractive – 12 **chequered** with a pattern of differently coloured squares – 12 **gesture** [ˈdʒestʃə] – 14 **staggered** shocked – 17 **to take s.o.** *here:* to move and surprise s.o. – 18 … **Two Thousand odd** … 2000 and a few years more – 23 **to let loose** to set free s.th. which has been held back – 23 **to suspend** to hold back for a period of time – 28 **rendering** performance, imitation – 28 **to withdraw a pace** to move back a step

carrying a chain of beautiful flowers altogether new to me, and put it about my neck. The idea was received with melodious applause; and presently they were all running to and fro for flowers, and laughingly flinging them upon me until I was almost
5 smothered with blossom. You who have never seen the like can scarcely imagine what delicate and wonderful flowers countless years of culture had created. Then someone suggested that their plaything should be exhibited in the nearest building, and so I was led past the sphinx of white marble, which had seemed to
10 watch me all the while with a smile at my astonishment, towards a vast grey edifice of fretted stone. As I went with them the memory of my confident anticipations of a profoundly grave and intellectual posterity came, with irresistible merriment, to my mind.

15   "The building had a huge entry, and was altogether of colossal dimensions. I was naturally most occupied with the growing crowd of little people, and with the big open portals that yawned before me shadowy and mysterious. My general impression of the world I saw over their heads was of a tangled waste of
20 beautiful bushes and flowers, a long-neglected and yet weedless garden. I saw a number of tall spikes of strange white flowers, measuring a foot perhaps across the spread of the waxen petals. They grew scattered, as if wild, among the variegated shrubs, but, as I say, I did not examine them closely at this time. The
25 Time Machine was left deserted on the turf among the rhododendrons.

    "The arch of the doorway was richly carved, but naturally I did not observe the carving very narrowly, though I fancied I saw suggestions of old Phoenician decorations as I passed

---

5 **to be smothered with** *here:* to be covered with – 5 **the like** anything like this –
7 **culture** *here:* cultivation – 8 **to exhibit** [-'--] to show in public – 11 **edifice** large
building – 11 **fretted** decorated with patterns – 12 **profoundly** thoroughly, extremely –
12 **grave** serious in manner – 13 **posterity** people and generations who live after one's
own time – 13 **merriment** laughter, cheerfulness – 19 **tangled** confused – 20 **weedless**
without any unwanted wild plants – 21 **spike** *here:* long, pointed group of flowers –
22 **petal** one of the leaf-like parts of a flower – 23 **variegated** many-coloured –
23 **shrub** low bush

through, and it struck me that they were very badly broken and weather-worn. Several more brightly clad people met me in the doorway, and so we entered, I, dressed in dingy nineteenth-century garments, looking grotesque enough, garlanded with
5 flowers, and surrounded by an eddying mass of bright, soft-coloured robes and shining white limbs, in a melodious whirl of laughter and laughing speech.

"The big doorway opened into a proportionately great hall hung with brown. The roof was in shadow, and the windows,
10 partially glazed with coloured glass and partially unglazed, admitted a tempered light. The floor was made up of huge blocks of some very hard white metal, not plates nor slabs, blocks, and it was so much worn, as I judged by the going to and fro of past generations, as to be deeply channelled along the more
15 frequented ways. Transverse to the length were innumerable tables made of slabs of polished stone, raised perhaps a foot from the floor, and upon these were heaps of fruits. Some I recognised as a kind of hypertrophied raspberry and orange, but for the most part they were strange.

20 "Between the tables was scattered a great number of cushions. Upon these my conductors seated themselves, signing for me to do likewise. With a pretty absence of ceremony they began to eat the fruit with their hands, flinging peel and stalks and so forth, into the round openings in the sides of the tables. I was
25 not loth to follow their example, for I felt thirsty and hungry. As I did so I surveyed the hall at my leisure.

---

3 **dingy** ['dɪndʒɪ] faded, dull, perhaps dirty – 4 **garlanded** hung with circles of flowers – 8 **proportionately** correspondingly – 10 **to glaze** to fit glass into – 11 **tempered** softened, moderate – 12 **slab** thick flat piece – 14 **channelled** hollowed out – 15 **frequented** [-'--] frequently used – 15 **transverse** at right angles – 18 **hypertrophied** [-'--] grown much bigger than the normal size – 18 **raspberry** small sweet red fruit *Himbeere* – 21 **conductor** *here:* person who leads s.o. – 23 **peel** outer covering of a fruit – 23 **stalk** the green part of a plant which supports a flower or fruit – 25 **to be loth** [ləʊθ] to be unwilling, to feel dislike – 26 **to survey** to look at – 26 **at leisure** without any hurry

"And perhaps the thing that struck me most was its dilapidated look. The stained-glass windows, which displayed only a geometrical pattern, were broken in many places, and the curtains that hung across the lower end were thick with dust.
5 And it caught my eye that the corner of the marble table near me was fractured. Nevertheless, the general effect was extremely rich and picturesque. There were, perhaps, a couple of hundred people dining in the hall, and most of them, seated as near to me as they could come, were watching me with interest, their
10 little eyes shining over the fruit they were eating. All were clad in the same soft, and yet strong, silky material.

"Fruit, by the bye, was all their diet. These people of the remote future were strict vegetarians, and while I was with them, in spite of some carnal cravings, I had to be frugivorous also. Indeed,
15 I found afterwards that horses, cattle, sheep, dogs, had followed the Ichthyosaurus into extinction. But the fruits were very delightful; one, in particular, that seemed to be in season all the time I was there — a floury thing in a three-sided husk — was especially good, and I made it my staple. At first I was puzzled
20 by all these strange fruits, and by the strange flowers I saw, but later I began to perceive their import.

"However, I am telling you of my fruit dinner in the distant future now. So soon as my appetite was a little checked, I determined to make a resolute attempt to learn the speech of
25 these new men of mine. Clearly that was the next thing to do. The fruits seemed a convenient thing to begin upon, and holding one of these up I began a series of interrogative sounds and gestures. I had some considerable difficulty in conveying my meaning. At first my efforts met with a stare of surprise or

---

1 **dilapidated** falling to pieces – 2 **stained-glass** of coloured glass – 6 **fractured** cracked, broken – 7 **picturesque** having the qualities of a painting – 12 **by the bye** by the way – 12 **diet** *here:* food – 14 **carnal cravings** hunger for meat – 14 **frugivorous** [fruːˈʤɪvərəs] feeding on fruit – 15 **to follow into extinction** die out like others before – 18 **floury** soft and powdery, like the powder used for making bread – 18 **husk** outer covering – 19 **staple** main food – 21 **to perceive** to understand – 21 **import** [ˈ--] meaning, importance

inextinguishable laughter, but presently a fair-haired little creature seemed to grasp my intention and repeated a name. They had to chatter and explain the business at great length to each other, and my first attempts to make the exquisite little

5   sounds of their language caused an immense amount of amusement. However, I felt like a schoolmaster amidst children, and persisted, and presently I had a score of noun substantives at least at my command; and then I got to demonstrative pronouns, and even the verb 'to eat'. But it was slow work, and

10 the little people soon tired and wanted to get away from my interrogations, so I determined, rather of necessity, to let them give their lessons in little doses when they felt inclined. And very little doses I found they were before long, for I never met people more indolent or more easily fatigued.

15   "A queer thing I soon discovered about my little hosts, and that was their lack of interest. They would come to me with eager cries of astonishment, like children, but like children they would soon stop examining me and wander away after some other toy. The dinner and my conversational beginnings ended,

20 I noted for the first time that almost all those who had surrounded me at first were gone. It is odd, too, how speedily I came to disregard these little people. I went out through the portal into the sunlit world again so soon as my hunger was satisfied. I was continually meeting more of these men of the future, who would

25 follow me a little distance, chatter and laugh about me, and, having smiled and gesticulated in a friendly way, leave me again to my own devices.

"The calm of evening was upon the world as I emerged from the great hall, and the scene was lit by the warm glow of the

30 setting sun. At first things were very confusing. Everything was so entirely different from the world I had known — even the

---

1 **inextinguishable** too great to be stopped – 6 **amidst** in the middle of – 7 **to persist** to continue to work at – 7 **score** twenty – 12 **to feel inclined** to wish to – 14 **indolent** lazy – 14 **fatigued** [fəˈtiːgd] tired – 15 **host** person who receives a guest – 22 **to disregard** to pay no attention to – 26 **to leave me to my own devices** to leave me alone

flowers. The big building I had left was situated on the slope of a broad river valley, but the Thames had shifted, perhaps, a mile from its present position. I resolved to mount to the summit of a crest, perhaps a mile and a half away, from which I could get a wider view of this our planet in the year Eight Hundred and Two Thousand Seven Hundred and One A.D. For that, I should explain, was the date the little dials of my machine recorded.

"As I walked I was watchful for every impression that could possibly help to explain the condition of ruinous splendour in which I found the world — for ruinous it was. A little way up the hill, for instance, was a great heap of granite, bound together by masses of aluminium, a vast labyrinth of precipitous walls and crumbled heaps, amidst which were thick heaps of very beautiful pagoda-like plants — nettles possibly — but wonderfully tinted with brown about the leaves, and incapable of stinging. It was evidently the derelict remains of some vast structure, to what end built I could not determine. It was here that I was destined, at a later date, to have a very strange experience — the first intimation of a still stranger discovery — but of that I will speak in its proper place.

"Looking round with a sudden thought, from a terrace on which I rested for a while, I realised that there were no small houses to be seen. Apparently the single house, and possibly even the household, had vanished. Here and there among the greenery were palace-like buildings, but the house and the cottage, which form such characteristic features of our own English landscape, had disappeared.

"'Communism,' said I to myself.

"And on the heels of that came another thought. I looked at the half dozen little figures that were following me. Then, in a

---

2 **to shift** to move, to change its position – 4 **crest** top of a hill – 9 **splendour** great beauty – 12 **precipitous** dangerously steep – 13 **crumbled** broken into small pieces – 14 **nettle** wild plant which makes the skin turn red when touched – 15 **tinted** delicately coloured – 15 **to sting, stung, stung** to cause sharp pain – 16 **derelict** left to fall to pieces – 16 **to what end** to what purpose – 19 **intimation** suggestion, hint

flash, I perceived that all had the same form of costume, the same soft hairless visage, and the same girlish rotundity of limb. It may seem strange, perhaps, that I had not noticed this before. But everything was so strange. Now, I saw the fact plainly enough. In costume, and in all the differences of texture and bearing that now mark off the sexes from each other, these people of the future were alike. And the children seemed to my eyes to be but the miniatures of their parents. I judged, then, that the children of that time were extremely precocious, physically at least, and I found afterwards abundant verification of my opinion.

"Seeing the ease and security in which these people were living, I felt that this close resemblance of the sexes was after all what one would expect; for the strength of a man and the softness of a woman, the institution of the family, and the differentiation of occupations are mere militant necessities of an age of physical force. Where population is balanced and abundant, much child-bearing becomes an evil rather than a blessing to the State; where violence comes but rarely and offspring are secure, there is less necessity — indeed there is no necessity — for an efficient family, and the specialisation of the sexes with reference to their children's needs disappears. We see some beginnings of this even in our own time, and in this future age it was complete. This, I must remind you, was my speculation at the time. Later, I was to appreciate how far it fell short of the reality.

"While I was musing upon these things, my attention was attracted by a pretty little structure, like a well under a cupola. I thought in a transitory way of the oddness of wells still existing, and then resumed the thread of my speculations. There were

---

2 **rotundity** roundness – 2 **limb** [lɪm] arm or leg – 5 **texture** *here:* constitution of the body – 9 **precocious** having developed earlier than is normal – 10 **abundant** more than enough – 15 **occupation** job, employment – 15 **militant** *here:* forcefully imposing itself – 19 **offspring** children – 24 **to appreciate** *here:* to understand fully – 24 **to fall short of s.th.** to fail to correspond to s.th. – 26 **to muse** to think deeply – 27 **well** hole for obtaining water from under the ground – 27 **to resume** to take up again – 29 **cupola** ['kjuːpələ] small rounded roof

no large buildings towards the top of the hill, and as my walking powers were evidently miraculous, I was presently left alone for the first time. With a strange sense of freedom and adventure I pushed on up to the crest.

5 "There I found a seat of some yellow metal that I did not recognise, corroded in places with a kind of pinkish rust and half smothered in soft moss, the arm rests cast and filed into the resemblance of griffins' heads. I sat down on it, and I surveyed the broad view of our old world under the sunset of that long
10 day. It was as sweet and fair a view as I have ever seen. The sun had already gone below the horizon and the west was flaming gold, touched with some horizontal bars of purple and crimson. Below was the valley of the Thames, in which the river lay like a band of burnished steel. I have already spoken of the great
15 palaces dotted about among the variegated greenery, some in ruins and some still occupied. Here and there rose a white or silvery figure in the waste garden of the earth, here and there came the sharp vertical line of some cupola or obelisk. There were no hedges, no signs of proprietary rights, no evidences of
20 agriculture; the whole earth had become a garden.

"So watching, I began to put my interpretation upon the things I had seen, and as it shaped itself to me that evening, my interpretation was something in this way. (Afterwards I found I had got only a half-truth — or only a glimpse of one facet of the
25 truth.)

"It seemed to me that I had happened upon humanity upon the wane. The ruddy sunset set me thinking of the sunset of mankind. For the first time I began to realise an odd consequence

---

2 **miraculous** very remarkable – 6 **to corrode** to destroy slowly – 6 **rust** reddish-brown coating on metals formed by water and air – 7 **moss** small green plants which grow on wet surfaces – 7 **arm rest** support for the arm – 7 **to cast, cast, cast** to pour very hot metal into a container to give it a certain shape – 8 **griffin** animal with a lion's body and the head and wings of an eagle – 12 **crimson** deep red – 14 **burnished** polished – 15 **dotted about** spread about at certain places – 19 **proprietary rights** rights of ownership – 24 **facet** ['fæsɪt] one of the many aspects of a thing – 26 **upon the wane** in the process of losing power and strength – 27 **ruddy** lit. red, reddish

of the social effort in which we are at present engaged. And yet, come to think, it is a logical consequence enough. Strength is the outcome of need; security sets a premium on feebleness. The work of ameliorating the conditions of life — the true
5 civilising process that makes life more and more secure — had gone steadily on to a climax. One triumph of a united humanity over Nature had followed another. Things that are now mere dreams had become projects deliberately put in hand and carried forward. And the harvest was what I saw!

10 "After all, the sanitation and the agriculture of today are still in the rudimentary stage. The science of our time has attacked but a little department of the field of human disease, but, even so, it spreads its operations very steadily and persistently. Our agriculture and horticulture destroy a weed just here and there
15 and cultivate perhaps a score or so of wholesome plants, leaving the greater number to fight out a balance as they can. We improve our favourite plants and animals — and how few they are — gradually by selective breeding; now a new and better peach, now a seedless grape, now a sweeter and larger flower, now a
20 more convenient breed of cattle. We improve them gradually, because our ideals are vague and tentative, and our knowledge is very limited; because Nature, too, is shy and slow in our clumsy hands. Some day all this will be better organised, and still better. That is the drift of the current in spite of the eddies. The whole
25 world will be intelligent, educated, and cooperating; things will move faster and faster towards the subjugation of Nature. In the end, wisely and carefully we shall readjust the balance of animal and vegetable life to suit our human needs.

---

3 **to set a premium on s.th.** to cause s.th. to be an advantage – 3 **feebleness** weakness – 4 **to ameliorate** to improve – 6 **climax** the most advanced point of a development – 8 **to put in hand** to start – 13 **operations** activities – 14 **horticulture** the science of growing fruit, flowers and vegetables – 15 **wholesome** healthy – 18 **selective breeding** growing certain plants and keeping certain animals while causing others to die out – 21 **tentative** *here:* formed in order to see the effect – 26 **subjugation** victory over, conquest of

"This adjustment, I say, must have been done, and done well; done indeed for all time, in the space of Time across which my machine had leaped. The air was free from gnats, the earth from weeds or fungi; everywhere were fruits and sweet and delightful
5 flowers; brilliant butterflies flew hither and thither. The ideal of preventive medicine was attained. Diseases had been stamped out. I saw no evidence of any contagious diseases during all my stay. And I shall have to tell you later that even the processes of putrefaction and decay had been profoundly affected by these
10 changes.

"Social triumphs, too, had been effected. I saw mankind housed in splendid shelters, gloriously clothed, and as yet I had found them engaged in no toil. There were no signs of struggle, neither social nor economical struggle. The shop, the
15 advertisement, traffic, all that commerce which constitutes the body of our world, was gone. It was natural on that golden evening that I should jump at the idea of a social paradise. The difficulty of increasing population had been met, I guessed, and population had ceased to increase.

20 "But with this change in condition comes inevitably adaptations to the change. What, unless biological science is a mass of errors, is the cause of human intelligence and vigour? Hardship and freedom: conditions under which the active, strong, and subtle survive and the weaker go to the wall;
25 conditions that put a premium upon the loyal alliance of capable men, upon self-restraint, patience, and decision. And the

3 **gnat** [næt] small fly that stings – 4 **fungus** (*pl.* fungi) plant without leaves or flowers, often growing on old wood – 5 **butterfly** insect with large beautifully coloured wings – 5 **hither and thither** *old use:* here and there, in all directions – 6 **to attain** to succeed in reaching – 7 **contagious** spreading from person to person by contact – 9 **putrefaction** the process of becoming rotten and ill-smelling – 9 **decay** going bad and/or losing strength – 13 **toil** *lit.* hard work – 14 **economical** *here:* economic – 15 **to constitute the body of s.th.** to be the main part of s.th. – 21 **adaptation** change so as to be suitable for different conditions – 22 **error** wrong idea – 22 **vigour** strength – 25 **alliance** close connection or association – 25 **capable** able, clever – 26 **self-restraint** self-control

institution of the family, and the emotions that arise therein, the fierce jealousy, the tenderness for offspring, parental self-devotion, all found their justification and support in the imminent dangers of the young. *Now,* where are these imminent

5 dangers? There is a sentiment arising, and it will grow, against connubial jealousy, against fierce maternity, against passion of all sorts; unnecessary things now, and things that make us uncomfortable, savage survivals, discords in a refined and pleasant life.

10 "I thought of the physical slightness of the people, their lack of intelligence, and those big abundant ruins, and it strengthened my belief in a perfect conquest of Nature. For after the battle comes Quiet. Humanity had been strong, energetic, and intelligent, and had used all its abundant vitality to alter the

15 conditions under which it lived. And now came the reaction of the altered conditions.

"Under the new conditions of perfect comfort and security, that restless energy, that with us is strength, would become weakness. Even in our own time certain tendencies and desires,

20 once necessary to survival, are a constant source of failure. Physical courage and the love of battle, for instance, are no great help — may even be hindrances — to a civilised man. And in a state of physical balance and security, power, intellectual as well as physical, would be out of place. For countless years I judged

25 there had been no danger of war or solitary violence, no danger from wild beasts, no wasting disease to require strength of constitution, no need of toil. For such a life, what we should call the weak are as well equipped as the strong, are indeed no longer weak. Better equipped indeed they are, for the strong would be

fretted by an energy for which there was no outlet. No doubt the exquisite beauty of the buildings I saw was the outcome of the last surgings of the now purposeless energy of mankind before it settled down into perfect harmony with the conditions
5 under which it lived — the flourish of that triumph which began the last great peace. This has ever been the fate of energy in security; it takes to art and to eroticism, and then come languor and decay.

"Even this artistic impetus would at last die away — had almost
10 died in the Time I saw. To adorn themselves with flowers, to dance, to sing in the sunlight; so much was left of the artistic spirit, and no more. Even that would fade in the end into a contented inactivity. We are kept keen on the grindstone of pain and necessity, and, it seemed to me, that here was that hateful
15 grindstone broken at last!

"As I stood there in the gathering dark I thought that in this simple explanation I had mastered the problem of the world — mastered the whole secret of these delicious people. Possibly the checks they had devised for the increase of population had
20 succeeded too well, and their numbers had rather diminished than kept stationary. That would account for the abandoned ruins. Very simple was my explanation, and plausible enough — as most wrong theories are!

5

25 "As I stood there musing over this too perfect triumph of man, the full moon, yellow and gibbous, came up out of an overflow of silver light in the north-east. The bright little figures ceased

---

1 **fretted** worried – 1 **outlet** way of using (one's energy, feelings, etc.) – 3 **to surge** to move forward in waves – 5 **flourish** *here:* ornamental expression – 7 **to take to** to turn to – 7 **languor** weakness, lack of life – 9 **impetus** impulse – 10 **to adorn** to decorate – 13 **keen** *here:* sharp – 13 **grindstone** round stone which is turned to sharpen knives – 14 **hateful** very unpleasant – 18 **delicious** *here:* delightful, pleasant – 21 **to keep stationary** to stay the same – 21 **to abandon** to desert, to go away not intending to return – 26 **gibbous** ['ɡɪbəs] with the bright part filling more than half a circle

to move about below, a noiseless owl flitted by, and I shivered with the chill of the night. I determined to descend and find where I could sleep.

"I looked for the building I knew. Then my eye travelled along to the figure of the White Sphinx upon the pedestal of bronze, growing distinct as the light of the rising moon grew brighter. I could see the silver birch against it. There was the tangle of rhododendron bushes, black in the pale light, and there was the little lawn. I looked at the lawn again. A queer doubt chilled my complacency. 'No,' said I stoutly to myself, 'that was not the lawn.'

"But it *was* the lawn. For the white leprous face of the sphinx was towards it. Can you imagine what I felt as this conviction came home to me? But you cannot. The Time Machine was gone!

"At once, like a lash across the face, came the possibility of losing my own age, of being left helpless in this strange new world. The bare thought of it was an actual physical sensation. I could feel it grip me at the throat and stop my breathing. In another moment I was in a passion of fear and running with great leaping strides down the slope. Once I fell headlong and cut my face; I lost no time in stanching the blood, but jumped up and ran on, with a warm trickle down my cheek and chin. All the time I ran I was saying to myself, 'They have moved it a little, pushed it under the bushes out of the way.' Nevertheless, I ran with all my might. All the time, with the certainty that sometimes comes with excessive dread, I knew that such assurance was folly, knew instinctively that the machine was removed out of my reach. My breath came with pain. I suppose I covered the whole distance from the hill crest to the little lawn,

---

1 **owl** night-flying bird with large eyes – 1 **to flit by** to fly past lightly and quickly –
2 **chill** coldness – 10 **complacency** feeling of quiet satisfaction – 10 **stout** *here:* brave –
12 **leprous** made silvery as if by the disease which causes the loss of fingers and
toes – 16 **lash** stroke with a whip – 21 **stride** long step – 22 **to stanch** to stop the flow
of – 23 **trickle** thin stream – 26 **might** strength – 28 **folly** foolishness

two miles, perhaps, in ten minutes. And I am not a young man. I cursed aloud, as I ran, at my confident folly in leaving the machine, wasting good breath thereby. I cried aloud, and none answered. Not a creature seemed to be stirring in that moonlit
5 world.

"When I reached the lawn my worst fears were realised. Not a trace of the thing was to be seen. I felt faint and cold when I faced the empty space among the black tangle of bushes. I ran round it furiously, as if the thing might be hidden in a corner,
10 and then stopped abruptly, with my hands clutching my hair. Above me towered the sphinx, upon the bronze pedestal, white, shining, leprous, in the light of the rising moon. It seemed to smile in mockery of my dismay.

"I might have consoled myself by imagining the little people
15 had put the mechanism in some shelter for me, had I not felt assured of their physical and intellectual inadequacy. That is what dismayed me: the sense of some hitherto unsuspected power, through whose intervention my invention had vanished. Yet, of one thing I felt assured: unless some other age had
20 produced its exact duplicate, the machine could not have moved in time. The attachment of the levers — I will show you the method later — prevented any one from tampering with it in that way when they were removed. It had moved, and was hid, only in space. But then, where could it be?

25 "I think I must have had a kind of frenzy. I remember running violently in and out among the moonlit bushes all round the sphinx, and startling some white animal that, in the dim light, I took for a small deer. I remember, too, late that night, beating the bushes with my clenched fists until my knuckles were gashed

2 **to curse** to swear, to use violent language – 9 **furious** full of violent excitement –
10 **to clutch** to hold tightly – 13 **in mockery of** laughing at – 13 **dismay** strong feeling of
fear and discouragement – 14 **to console o.s.** to find comfort – 15 **shelter** s.th. that
gives safety or protection – 16 **inadequacy** weakness – 17 **unsuspected** which I had not
believed to exist – 22 **to tamper with** to play around with s.th. without permission –
28 **deer** quick-running animal, the male of which has horns – 29 **knuckles** bones at the
finger-joints – 29 **gashed** cut deeply

and bleeding from the broken twigs. Then, sobbing and raving in my anguish of mind, I went down to the great building of stone. The big hall was dark, silent, and deserted. I slipped on the uneven floor, and fell over one of the malachite tables, almost
5 breaking my shin. I lit a match and went on past the dusty curtains, of which I have told you.

"There I found a second great hall covered with cushions, upon which, perhaps, a score or so of the little people were sleeping. I have no doubt they found my second appearance
10 strange enough, coming suddenly out of the quiet darkness with inarticulate noises and the splutter and flare of a match. For they had forgotten about matches. 'Where is my Time Machine?' I began, bawling like an angry child, laying hands upon them and shaking them up together. It must have been very queer to
15 them. Some laughed, most of them looked sorely frightened. When I saw them standing round me, it came into my head that I was doing as foolish a thing as it was possible for me to do under the circumstances, in trying to revive the sensation of fear. For, reasoning from their daylight behaviour, I thought that
20 fear must be forgotten.

"Abruptly, I dashed down the match, and, knocking one of the people over in my course, went blundering across the big dining-hall again, out under the moonlight. I heard cries of terror and their little feet running and stumbling this way and that. I do
25 not remember all I did as the moon crept up the sky. I suppose it was the unexpected nature of my loss that maddened me. I felt hopelessly cut off from my own kind — a strange animal in an unknown world. I must have raved to and fro, screaming and crying upon God and Fate. I have a memory of horrible fatigue,

1 **twig** small branch – 1 **to sob** to weep loudly and irregularly – 1 **to rave** to talk wildly as if mad – 2 **anguish** great suffering – 4 **malachite** ['mæləkaıt] green stone used for decoration – 5 **shin** front part of the leg below the knee – 11 **inarticulate** not clear enough to be understood – 11 **splutter** light explosive noise – 11 **flare** bright unsteady flame – 13 **to bawl** to shout or cry loudly – 18 **to revive** to bring back into existence – 21 **to dash down** to throw down with great force – 22 **to blunder** to move unsteadily as if blind – 24 **to stumble** to blunder and almost fall

as the long night of despair wore away; of looking in this impossible place and that; of groping among moonlit ruins and touching strange creatures in the black shadows; at last, of lying on the ground near the sphinx and weeping with absolute
5 wretchedness. I had nothing left but misery. Then I slept, and when I woke again it was full day, and a couple of sparrows were hopping round me on the turf within reach of my arm.

"I sat up in the freshness of the morning, trying to remember how I had got there, and why I had such a profound sense of
10 desertion and despair. Then things came clear in my mind. With the plain, reasonable daylight, I could look my circumstances fairly in the face. I saw the wild folly of my frenzy overnight, and I could reason with myself. Suppose the worst? I said. Suppose the machine altogether lost — perhaps destroyed? It behoves
15 me to be calm and patient, to learn the way of the people, to get a clear idea of the method of my loss, and the means of getting materials and tools; so that in the end, perhaps, I may make another. That would be my only hope, a poor hope perhaps, but better than despair. And, after all, it was a beautiful and
20 curious world.

"But probably the machine had only been taken away. Still, I must be calm and patient, find its hiding-place, and recover it by force or cunning. And with that I scrambled to my feet and looked about me, wondering where I could bathe. I felt weary,
25 stiff, and travel-soiled. The freshness of the morning made me desire an equal freshness. I had exhausted my emotion. Indeed, as I went about my business, I found myself wondering at my intense excitement overnight. I made a careful examination of the ground about the little lawn. I wasted some time in futile
30 questionings, conveyed, as well as I was able, to such of the little people as came by. They all failed to understand my gestures; some were simply stolid, some thought it was a jest and laughed

2 **to grope** to feel and search as in the dark – 5 **wretchedness** misery –
11 **circumstances** situation – 14 **it behoves me** *old use:* it is necessary for me –
23 **cunning** a clever trick – 23 **to scramble** to struggle – 29 **futile** useless, unsuccessful –
32 **stolid** completely unmoved – 32 **jest** joke

at me. I had the hardest task in the world to keep my hands off their pretty laughing faces. It was a foolish impulse, but the devil begotten of fear and blind anger was ill curbed and still eager to take advantage of my perplexity. The turf gave better counsel. I found a groove ripped in it, about midway between the pedestal of the sphinx and the marks of my feet where, on arrival, I had struggled with the overturned machine. There were other signs of removal about, with queer narrow footprints like those I could imagine made by a sloth. This directed my closer attention to the pedestal. It was, as I think I have said, of bronze. It was not a mere block, but highly decorated with deep framed panels on either side. I went and rapped at these. The pedestal was hollow. Examining the panels with care I found them discontinuous with the frames. There were no handles or keyholes, but possibly the panels, if they were doors, as I supposed, opened from within. One thing was clear enough to my mind. It took no very great mental effort to infer that my Time Machine was inside that pedestal. But how it got there was a different problem.

"I saw the heads of two orange-clad people coming through the bushes and under some blossom-covered apple-trees towards me. I turned smiling to them and beckoned them to me. They came, and then, pointing to the bronze pedestal, I tried to intimate my wish to open it. But at my first gesture towards this they behaved very oddly. I don't know how to convey their expression to you. Suppose you were to use a grossly improper gesture to a delicate-minded woman — it is how she would look. They went off as if they had received the last possible insult. I tried a sweet-looking little chap in white next, with exactly the same result. Somehow, his manner made me feel

3 **to beget, begot, begotten** *lit.* to be the cause of – 3 **ill curbed** badly controlled – 4 **perplexity** confusion – 4 **counsel** advice, information – 5 **groove** long hollow channel – 5 **to rip** to tear violently – 9 **sloth** [sləʊθ] American animal which lives in trees and moves very slowly – 12 **to rap** to strike lightly – 13 **discontinuous** not of one piece – 17 **to infer** to conclude – 21 **to beckon** to call s.o. by a movement of the hand – 23 **to intimate** ['ɪntɪmeɪt] to express, to convey – 25 **grossly** ['grəʊslɪ] totally – 26 **improper** vulgar

ashamed of myself. But, as you know, I wanted the Time Machine, and I tried him once more. As he turned off, like the others, my temper got the better of me. In three strides I was after him, had him by the loose part of his robe round the neck, and began dragging him towards the sphinx. Then I saw the horror and repugnance of his face, and all of a sudden I let him go.

"But I was not beaten yet. I banged with my fist at the bronze panels. I thought I heard something stir inside — to be explicit, I thought I heard a sound like a chuckle — but I must have been mistaken. Then I got a big pebble from the river, and came and hammered till I had flattened a coil in the decorations, and the verdigris came off in powdery flakes. The delicate little people must have heard me hammering in gusty outbreaks a mile away on either hand, but nothing came of it. I saw a crowd of them upon the slopes, looking furtively at me. At last, hot and tired, I sat down to watch the place. But I was too restless to watch long; I am too Occidental for a long vigil. I could work at a problem for years, but to wait inactive for twenty-four hours — that is another matter.

"I got up after a time, and began walking aimlessly through the bushes towards the hill again. 'Patience,' said I to myself. 'If you want your machine again you must leave that sphinx alone. If they mean to take your machine away, it's little good your wrecking their bronze panels, and if they don't, you will get it back as soon as you can ask for it. To sit among all those unknown things before a puzzle like that is hopeless. That way lies monomania. Face this world. Learn its ways, watch it, be careful of too hasty guesses at its meaning. In the end you will find clues to it all.' Then suddenly the humour of the situation came into

---

3 **to get the better of s.o.** to overcome s.o. – 5 **to drag** to pull – 6 **repugnance** strong dislike – 9 **to stir** to move – 10 **chuckle** quiet laugh – 11 **pebble** round stone – 12 **coil** spiral – 14 **gusty** sudden and violent – 16 **furtively** secretly, not directly – 18 **Occidental** belonging to the western world – 18 **vigil** watching and waiting – 28 **monomania** being occupied by one idea or subject only – 29 **clue** s.th. that suggests an answer to a problem

my mind: the thought of the years I had spent in study and toil to get into the future age, and now my passion of anxiety to get out of it. I had made myself the most complicated and the most hopeless trap that ever a man devised. Although it was at my own expense, I could not help myself. I laughed aloud.

"Going through the big palace, it seemed to me that the little people avoided me. It may have been my fancy, or it may have had something to do with my hammering at the gates of bronze. Yet I felt tolerably sure of the avoidance. I was careful, however, to show no concern and to abstain from any pursuit of them, and in the course of a day or two things got back to the old footing. I made what progress I could in the language, and in addition I pushed my explorations here and there. Either I missed some subtle point, or their language was excessively simple — almost exclusively composed of concrete substantives and verbs. There seemed to be few, if any, abstract terms, or little use of figurative language. Their sentences were usually simple and of two words, and I failed to convey or understand any but the simplest propositions. I determined to put the thought of my Time Machine and the mystery of the bronze doors under the sphinx as much as possible in a corner of memory, until my growing knowledge would lead me back to them in a natural way. Yet a certain feeling, you may understand, tethered me in a circle of a few miles round the point of my arrival.

"So far as I could see, all the world displayed the same exuberant richness as the Thames valley. From every hill I climbed I saw the same abundance of splendid buildings, endlessly varied in material and style, the same clustering thickets of evergreens, the same blossom-laden trees and tree-ferns. Here and there water shone like silver, and beyond, the

9 **tolerably** fairly – 10 **to abstain from** to hold oneself back from – 12 **footing** relationship – 17 **figurative** metaphorical, imaginative – 19 **proposition** *here:* statement, sentence – 23 **to tether** to fasten as if by a rope or chain – 26 **exuberant** overflowing – 28 **clustering** growing close together – 29 **thicket** thick growth of bushes and small trees – 29 **fern** feathery green-leaved flowerless plant

land rose into blue undulating hills, and so faded into the serenity of the sky. A peculiar feature, which presently attracted my attention, was the presence of certain circular wells, several, as it seemed to me, of a very great depth. One lay by the path up the hill, which I had followed during my first walk. Like the others, it was rimmed with bronze, curiously wrought, and protected by a little cupola from the rain. Sitting by the side of these wells, and peering down into the shafted darkness, I could see no gleam of water, nor could I start any reflection with a lighted match. But in all of them I heard a certain sound: a thud — thud — thud, like the beating of some big engine; and I discovered, from the flaring of my matches, that a steady current of air set down the shafts. Further, I threw a scrap of paper into the throat of one, and, instead of fluttering slowly down, it was at once sucked swiftly out of sight.

"After a time, too, I came to connect these wells with tall towers standing here and there upon the slopes; for above them there was often just such a flicker in the air as one sees on a hot day above a sun-scorched beach. Putting things together, I reached a strong suggestion of an extensive system of subterranean ventilation, whose true import it was difficult to imagine. I was at first inclined to associate it with the sanitary apparatus of these people. It was an obvious conclusion, but it was absolutely wrong.

"And here I must admit that I learned very little of drains and bells and modes of conveyance, and the like conveniences, during my time in this real future. In some of these visions of Utopias and coming times which I have read, there is a vast

---

1 **undulating** rising and falling like waves – 1 **serenity** cloudless calm – 6 **rimmed** covered at the edge – 6 **wrought** worked into shape – 9 **gleam** *here:* soft light, especially one that moves – 9 **reflection** light thrown back as if by a mirror – 13 **to set down** *here:* to move down – 13 **scrap** bit, piece – 15 **to suck** to draw – 19 **sun-scorched** heated by the sun – 20 **subterranean** underground – 25 **drains** system of pipes to carry away dirty water – 26 **mode of conveyance** means of transport – 28 **Utopia** ideal society

amount of detail about building, and social arrangements, and so forth. But while such details are easy enough to obtain when the whole world is contained in one's imagination, they are altogether inaccessible to a real traveller amid such realities as
5 I found here. Conceive the tale of London which a negro, fresh from Central Africa, would take back to his tribe! What would he know of railway companies, of social movements, of telephone and telegraph wires, of the Parcels Delivery Company, and postal orders and the like? Yet we, at least, should be willing enough
10 to explain these things to him! And even of what he knew, how much could he make his untravelled friend either apprehend or believe? Then, think how narrow the gap between a negro and a white man of our own times, and how wide the interval between myself and these of the Golden Age! I was sensible of
15 much which was unseen, and which contributed to my comfort; but save for a general impression of automatic organisation, I fear I can convey very little of the difference to your mind.

"In the matter of sepulture, for instance, I could see no signs of crematoria nor anything suggestive of tombs. But it occured
20 to me that, possibly, there might be cemeteries (or crematoria) somewhere beyond the range of my explorings. This, again, was a question I deliberately put to myself, and my curiosity was at first entirely defeated upon the point. The thing puzzled me, and I was led to make a further remark, which puzzled me still
25 more: that aged and infirm among this people there were none.

"I must confess that my satisfaction with my first theories of an automatic civilisation and a decadent humanity did not long endure. Yet I could think of no other. Let me put my difficulties.

---

4 **inaccessible** unable to be – 8 **postal order** way of paying money through a post office – 11 **to apprehend** *old use:* to understand – 14 **Golden Age** (from Greek mythology) happiest period in history – 14 **sensible** *here:* aware – 18 **sepulture** [ˈsepltʃə] burying of the dead – 19 **tomb** [tuːm] grave, especially one with a monument – 20 **cemetery** ground for burying dead people – 25 **aged** [ˈeɪdʒɪd] very old people – 25 **infirm** weak in body and mind

The several big palaces I had explored were mere living places, great dining-halls and sleeping apartments. I could find no machinery, no appliances of any kind. Yet these people were clothed in pleasant fabrics that must at times need renewal, and

5 their sandals, though undecorated, were fairly complex specimens of metal-work. Somehow such things must be made. And the little people displayed no vestige of a creative tendency. There were, no shops, no workshops, no sign of importations among them. They spent all their time in playing gently, in

10 bathing in the river, in making love in a half-playful fashion, in eating fruit and sleeping. I could not see how things were kept going.

"Then, again, about the Time Machine: something, I knew not what, had taken it into the hollow pedestal of the White

15 Sphinx. *Why?* For the life of me I could not imagine. Those waterless wells, too, those flickering pillars. I felt I lacked a clue. I felt — how shall I put it? Suppose you found an inscription, with sentences here and there in excellent plain English, and, interpolated therewith, others made up of words, of letters even,

20 absolutely unknown to you? Well, on the third day of my visit, that was how the world of Eight Hundred and Two Thousand Seven Hundred and One presented itself to me!

"That day, too, I made a friend — of a sort. It happened that, as I was watching some of the little people bathing in a shallow,

25 one of them was seized with cramp and began drifting downstream. The main current ran rather swiftly, but not too strongly for even a moderate swimmer. It will give you an idea, therefore, of the strange deficiency in these creatures, when I

---

3 **appliance** instrument or mechanism – 4 **fabrics** kinds of cloth – 6 **specimen** example – 7 **vestige** remains, trace – 8 **importation** s.th. that has been imported – 10 **to make love** to kiss, to caress, etc. – 15 **For the life of me** However hard I tried – 16 **pillar** tower or column – 17 **inscription** piece of writing on a stone – 19 **interpolated** added, mixed – 24 **shallow** part of a river that is not deep – 25 **cramp** painful tightening of a muscle – 28 **deficiency** imperfection, weakness

tell you that none made the slightest attempt to rescue the weakly crying little thing which was drowning before their eyes. When I realised this, I hurriedly slipped off my clothes, and, wading in at a point lower down, I caught the poor mite and
5   drew her safe to land. A little rubbing of the limbs soon brought her round, and I had the satisfaction of seeing she was all right before I left her. I had got to such a low estimate of her kind that I did not expect any gratitude from her. In that, however, I was wrong.

10   "This happened in the morning. In the afternoon I met my little woman, as I believe it was, as I was returning towards my centre from an exploration, and she received me with cries of delight and presented me with a big garland of flowers — evidently made for me and me alone. The thing took my
15   imagination. Very possibly I had been feeling desolate. At any rate I did my best to display my appreciation of the gift. We were soon seated together in a little stone arbour, engaged in conversation, chiefly of smiles. The creature's friendliness affected me exactly as a child's might have done. We passed
20   each other flowers, and she kissed my hands. I did the same to hers. Then I tried talk, and found that her name was Weena, which, though I don't know what it meant, somehow seemed appropriate enough. That was the beginning of a queer friendship which lasted a week, and ended — as I will tell you!

25   "She was exactly like a child. She wanted to be with me always. She tried to follow me everywhere, and on my next journey out and about it went to my heart to tire her down, and leave her at last, exhausted and calling after me rather plaintively. But the problems of the world had to be mastered. I had not, I said to
30   myself, come into the future to carry on a miniature flirtation.

4 **mite** s.th. small, especially a child –5 **to bring s.o. round** to make s.o. become
conscious again – 7 **estimate** *here:* opinion – 8 **gratitude** thankfulness – 15 **desolate**
sad and lonely – 16 **appreciation** *here:* thankful feelings – 17 **arbour** shady place in a
garden with plants growing over a framework – 17 **engaged in** busy with –
23 **appropriate** suitable – 28 **exhausted** extremely tired – 28 **plaintively** sadly,
pitifully – 30 **flirtation** showing love for s.o. without serious intentions

Yet her distress when I left her was very great, her expostulations at the parting were sometimes frantic, and I think, altogether, I had as much trouble as comfort from her devotion. Nevertheless she was, somehow, a very great comfort. I thought it was mere
5 childish affection that made her cling to me. Until it was too late, I did not clearly know what I had inflicted upon her when I left her. Nor until it was too late did I clearly understand what she was to me. For, by merely seeming fond of me, and showing in her weak, futile way that she cared for me, the little doll of a
10 creature presently gave my return to the neighbourhood of the White Sphinx almost the feeling of coming home; and I would watch for her tiny figure of white and gold so soon as I came over the hill.

"It was from her, too, that I learned that fear had not yet left
15 the world. She was fearless enough in the daylight, and she had the oddest confidence in me; for once, in a foolish moment, I made threatening grimaces at her, and she simply laughed at them. But she dreaded the dark, dreaded shadows, dreaded black things. Darkness to her was the one thing dreadful. It was
20 a singularly passionate emotion, and it set me thinking and observing. I discovered then, among other things, that these little people gathered into the great houses after dark, and slept in droves. To enter upon them without a light was to put them into a tumult of apprehension. I never found one out of doors,
25 or one sleeping alone within doors, after dark. Yet I was still such a blockhead that I missed the lesson of that fear, and in spite of Weena's distress, I insisted upon sleeping away from these slumbering multitudes.

"It troubled her greatly, but in the end her odd affection for
30 me triumphed, and for five of the nights of our acquaintance, including the last night of all, she slept with her head pillowed

---

1 **expostulation** complaint, protest – 5 **affection** fondness – 5 **to cling, clung, clung** to refuse to let go – 6 **to inflict s.th. upon s.o.** to make s.o. suffer – 12 **tiny** extremely small – 23 **drove** group, crowd – 24 **apprehension** fear – 26 **blockhead** slow and stupid person – 28 **to slumber** to sleep

on my arm. But my story slips away from me as I speak of her. It must have been the night before her rescue that I was awakened about dawn. I had been restless, dreaming most disagreeably that I was drowned, and that sea-anemones were feeling over my face with their soft palps. I woke with a start, and with an odd fancy that some greyish animal had just rushed out of the chamber. I tried to get to sleep again, but I felt restless and uncomfortable. It was that dim grey hour when things are just creeping out of darkness, when everything is colourless and clear cut, and yet unreal. I got up, and went down into the great hall, and so out upon the flagstones in front of the palace. I thought I would make a virtue of necessity, and see the sunrise.

"The moon was setting, and the dying moonlight and the first pallor of dawn were mingled in a ghastly half-light. The bushes were inky black, the ground a sombre grey, the sky colourless and cheerless. And up the hill I thought I could see ghosts. Three several times, as I scanned the slope, I saw white figures. Twice I fancied I saw a solitary white, ape-like creature running rather quickly up the hill, and once near the ruins I saw a leash of them carrying some dark body. They moved hastily. I did not see what became of them. It seemed that they vanished among the bushes. The dawn was still indistinct, you must understand.

I was feeling that chill, uncertain, early-morning feeling you may have known. I doubted my eyes.

"As the eastern sky grew brighter, and the light of the day came on and its vivid colouring returned upon the world once more, I scanned the view keenly. But I saw no vestige of my white figures. They were mere creatures of the half-light. 'They must have been ghosts,' I said; 'I wonder whence they dated.' For a

---

3 **dawn** daybreak – 4 **disagreeably** unpleasantly – 4 **sea-anemone** [ˈsiːəˌnemənɪ] – 5 **palp** arm for feeling with – 11 **flagstone** flat stone for a floor or path – 15 **pallor** paleness – 15 **to mingle** to mix – 16 **sombre** dark – 17 **cheerless** dull, miserable – 18 **to scan** to examine, to search – 20 **a leash** three – 30 **whence** *old use:* from when

queer notion of Grant Allen's came into my head, and amused
me. If each generation die and leave ghosts, he argued, the world
at last will get overcrowded with them. On that theory they would
have grown innumerable some Eight Hundred Thousand Years
5 hence, and it was no great wonder to see four at once. But the
jest was unsatisfying, and I was thinking of these figures all the
morning, until Weena's rescue drove them out of my head. I
associated them in some indefinite way with the white animal
I had startled in my first passionate search for the Time Machine.
10 But Weena was a pleasant substitute. Yet all the same, they were
soon destined to take far deadlier possession of my mind.

"I think I have said how much hotter than our own was the
weather of this Golden Age. I cannot account for it. It may be
that the sun was hotter, or the earth nearer the sun. It is usual
15 to assume that the sun will go on cooling steadily in the future.
But people, unfamiliar with such speculations as those of the
younger Darwin, forget that the planets must ultimately fall back
one by one into the parent body. As these catastrophes occur,
the sun will blaze with renewed energy; and it may be that some
20 inner planet had suffered this fate. Whatever the reason, the fact
remains that the sun was very much hotter than we know it.

"Well, one very hot morning — my fourth, I think — as I was
seeking shelter from the heat and glare in a colossal ruin near
the great house where I slept and fed, there happened this strange
25 thing: Clambering among these heaps of masonry, I found a
narrow gallery, whose end and side windows were blocked by
fallen masses of stone. By contrast with the brilliancy outside,
it seemed at first impenetrably dark to me. I entered it groping,
for the change from light to blackness made spots of colour

---

1 **notion** idea – 1 **Grant Allen** a late-nineteenth-century philosophical writer and
novelist (1848–99) – 15 **to assume** to suppose – 17 **the younger Darwin** Charles Robert
Darwin (1809–82), the author of *On the Origin of Species,* whose grandfather was
Erasmus Darwin (1731–1802), the naturalist and poet – 18 **parent body** *here:* the
original star from which they (the planets) – 19 **to blaze** to burn or shine brightly –
25 **masonry** *here:* stones and broken walls – 26 **gallery** long, narrow room or hall –
28 **impenetrable** too dark to see or walk through

swim before me. Suddenly I halted spellbound. A pair of eyes, luminous by reflection against the daylight without, was watching me out of the darkness.

"The old instinctive dread of wild beasts came upon me. I
5 clenched my hands and steadfastly looked into the glaring eyeballs. I was afraid to turn. Then the thought of the absolute security in which humanity appeared to be living came to my mind. And then I remembered that strange terror of the dark. Overcoming my fear to some extent, I advanced a step and
10 spoke. I will admit that my voice was harsh and ill-controlled. I put out my hand and touched something soft. At once the eyes darted sideways, and something white ran past me. I turned with my heart in my mouth, and saw a queer little ape-like figure, its head held down in a peculiar manner, running across the
15 sunlit space behind me. It blundered against a block of granite, staggered aside, and in a moment was hidden in a black shadow beneath another pile of ruined masonry.

"My impression of it is, of course, imperfect; but I know it was a dull white, and had strange large greyish-red eyes; also that
20 there was flaxen hair on its head and down its back. But, as I say, it went too fast for me to see distinctly. I cannot even say whether it ran on all fours, or only with its forearms held very low. After an instant's pause I followed it into the second heap of ruins. I could not find it at first; but, after a time in the
25 profound obscurity, I came upon one of those round well-like openings of which I have told you, half closed by a fallen pillar. A sudden thought came to me. Could this Thing have vanished down the shaft? I lit a match, and, looking down, I saw a small, white, moving creature, with large bright eyes which regarded
30 me steadfastly as it retreated. It made me shudder. It was so like a human spider! It was clambering down the wall, and now I saw for the first time a number of metal foot and hand rests

---

1 **spellbound** fascinated – 12 **to dart** to move suddenly and quickly – 13 **with my heart in my mouth** very afraid and worried – 20 **flaxen** pale yellow – 25 **obscurity** darkness

forming a kind of ladder down the shaft. Then the light burned my fingers and fell out of my hand, going out as it dropped, and when I had lit another the little monster had disappeared.

"I do not know how long I sat peering down that well. It was
5 not for some time that I could succeed in persuading myself that the thing I had seen was human. But, gradually, the truth dawned on me: that Man had not remained one species, but had differentiated into two distinct animals: that my graceful children of the Upperworld were not the sole descendants of
10 our generation, but that this bleached, obscene, nocturnal Thing, which had flashed before me, was also heir to all the ages.

"I thought of the flickering pillars and of my theory of an underground ventilation. I began to suspect their true import. And what, I wondered, was this Lemur doing in my scheme of
15 a perfectly balanced organisation? How was it related to the indolent serenity of the beautiful Upperworlders? And what was hidden down there, at the foot of that shaft? I sat upon the edge of the well telling myself that, at any rate, there was nothing to fear, and that there I must descend for the solution
20 of my difficulties. And withal I was absolutely afraid to go! As I hesitated, two of the beautiful Upperworld people came running in their amorous sport across the daylight into the shadow. The male pursued the female, flinging flowers at her as he ran.

"They seemed distressed to find me, my arm against the
25 overturned pillar, peering down the well. Apparently it was considered bad form to remark these apertures; for when I pointed to this one, and tried to frame a question about it in their tongue, they were still more visibly distressed and turned away. But they were interested by my matches, and I struck some

---

7 **species** ['spiːʃiːz] group that has common characteristics – 9 **sole** only – 10 **to bleach** to make or become white – 10 **nocturnal** active at night – 11 **all the ages** *here:* all the periods of history and generations of men that had come before – 14 **Lemur** ['liːmə] monkey-like animal that is active at night – 14 **scheme** [skiːm] system – 20 **withal** *old use:* besides – 22 **amorous sport** love games – 23 **to pursue** to follow, to try to catch – 26 **aperture** ['æpəˌtjʊə] hole, opening

to amuse them. I tried them again about the well, and again I
failed. So presently I left them, meaning to go back to Weena,
and see what I could get from her. But my mind was already in
revolution; my guesses and impressions were slipping and
5 sliding to a new adjustment. I had now a clue to the import of
these wells, to the ventilating towers, to the mystery of the ghosts;
to say nothing of a hint at the meaning of the bronze gates and
the fate of the Time Machine! And very vaguely there came a
suggestion towards the solution of the economic problem that
10 had puzzled me.

"Here was the new view. Plainly, this second species of Man
was subterranean. There were three circumstances in particular
which made me think that its rare emergence above ground was
the outcome of a long-continued underground habit. In the first
15 place, there was the bleached look common in most animals
that live largely in the dark — the white fish of the Kentucky
caves, for instance. Then, those large eyes, with that capacity
for reflecting light, are common features of nocturnal things
— witness the owl and the cat. And last of all, that evident
20 confusion in the sunshine, that hasty yet fumbling and awkward
flight towards dark shadow, and that peculiar carriage of the
head while in the light — all reinforced the theory of an extreme
sensitiveness of the retina.

"Beneath my feet, then, the earth must be tunnelled
25 enormously, and these tunnellings were the habitat of the new
race. The presence of ventilating-shafts and wells along the hill
slopes — everywhere, in fact, except along the river valley —
showed how universal were its ramifications. What so natural,

---

4 **in revolution** *here:* in the process of complete change – 5 **adjustment** *here:* order,
system – 13 **emergence** coming up – 17 **cave** a hollow place in a cliff or under the
ground – 17 **capacity** ability – 20 **fumbling** moving clumsily and nervously –
20 **awkward** clumsy – 21 **carriage** *here:* way of carrying – 22 **to reinforce** to strengthen,
to support – 23 **sensitiveness** quickly or easily receiving impressions – 23 **retina**
light-sensitive area of nerve-endings at the back of the eye – 25 **habitat** home –
28 **ramification** branch or part of a system

then, as to assume that it was in this artificial Underworld that such work as was necessary to the comfort of the daylight race was done? The notion was so plausible that I at once accepted it, and went on to assume the *how* of this splitting of the human species. I dare say you will anticipate the shape of my theory; though, for myself, I very soon felt that it fell far short of the truth.

"At first, proceeding from the problems of our own age, it seemed clear as daylight to me that the gradual widening of the present merely temporary and social difference between the Capitalist and the Labourer, was the key to the whole position. No doubt it will seem grotesque enough to you — and wildly incredible! — and yet even now there are existing circumstances to point that way. There is a tendency to utilise underground space for the less ornamental purposes of civilisation; there is the Metropolitan Railway in London, for instance, there are new electric railways, there are subways, there are underground workrooms and restaurants, and they increase and multiply. Evidently, I thought, this tendency had increased till industry had gradually lost its birthright in the sky. I mean that it had gone deeper and deeper into larger and ever larger underground factories, spending a still-increasing amount of its time therein, till, in the end—! Even now, does not an East-end worker live in such artificial conditions as practically to be cut off from the natural surface of the earth?

"Again, the exclusive tendency of richer people — due, not doubt, to the increasing refinement of their education, and the widening gulf between them and the rude violence of the poor — is already leading to the closing, in their interest, of considerable portions of the surface of the land. About London,

---

1 **artificial** not natural, made for a special purpose – 4 **to split, split, split** to divide – 14 **to utilise** to use – 16 **Metropolitan Railway** the first London underground railway, which dates back to 1863 – 17 **subway** path under a road or railway – 20 **birthright in the sky** *here:* traditional right of existing above ground – 27 **refinement** removal of everything that is ugly or indelicate – 28 **gulf** difference, division

for instance, perhaps half the prettier country is shut in against intrusion. And this same widening gulf — which is due to the length and expense of the higher educational process and the increased facilities for and temptations towards refined habits

5 on the part of the rich — will make that exchange between class and class, that promotion by intermarriage which at present retards the splitting of our species along lines of social stratification, less and less frequent. So, in the end, above ground you must have the Haves, pursuing pleasure and comfort, and

10 beauty, and below ground the Have-nots, the Workers getting continually adapted to the conditions of their labour. Once they were there, they would no doubt have to pay rent, and not a little of it, for the ventilation of their caverns; and if they refused, they would starve or be suffocated for arrears. Such of them as

15 were so constituted as to be miserable and rebellious would die; and, in the end, the balance being permanent, the survivors would become as well adapted to the conditions of underground life, and as happy in their way, as the Upperworld people were to theirs. As it seemed to me, the refined beauty and the etiolated

20 pallor followed naturally enough.

"The great triumph of Humanity I had dreamed of took a different shape in my mind. It had been no such triumph of moral education and general cooperation as I had imagined. Instead, I saw a real aristocracy, armed with a perfected science

25 and working to a logical conclusion the industrial system of today. Its triumph had not been simply a triumph over Nature, but a triumph over Nature and the fellow man. This, I must warn you, was my theory at the time. I had no convenient cicerone

---

2 **intrusion** *here:* entering private property without permission – 4 **facilities** means – 4 **temptation towards** attraction of – 6 **promotion** advancement in social rank – 6 **intermarriage** *here:* marriage between members of different classes – 7 **to retard** to slow down – 8 **stratification** *here:* different social levels, strata or classes – 9 **the Haves** [hævz] the rich – 10 **the Have-nots** the poor – 13 **cavern** large cave – 14 **to suffocate** to let s.o. die through lack of air – 14 **arrears** rent that should have been paid but has not yet been paid – 19 **etiolated** ['iːtɪəleɪtɪd] white or pale as a result of being kept in the dark – 28 **cicerone** [ˌsɪsəˈrəʊnɪ] *lit.* guide

in the pattern of the Utopian books. My explanation may be absolutely wrong. I still think it is the most plausible one. But even on this supposition the balanced civilisation that was at last attained must have long since passed its zenith, and
5 was now far fallen into decay. The too-perfect security of the Upperworlders had led them to a slow movement of degeneration, to a general dwindling in size, strength, and intelligence. That I could see clearly enough already. What had happened to the Undergrounders I did not yet suspect; but,
10 from what I had seen of the Morlocks — that, by the bye, was the name by which these creatures were called — I could imagine that the modification of the human type was even far more profound than among the 'Eloi,' the beautiful race that I already knew.

15   "Then came troublesome doubts. Why had the Morlocks taken my Time Machine? For I felt sure it was they who had taken it. Why, too, if the Eloi were masters, could they not restore the machine to me? And why were they so terribly afraid of the dark? I proceeded, as I have said, to question Weena about this
20 Underworld, but here again I was disappointed. At first she would not understand my questions, and presently she refused to answer them. She shivered as though the topic was unendurable. And when I pressed her, perhaps a little harshly, she burst into tears. They were the only tears, except my own,
25 I ever saw in that Golden Age. When I saw them I ceased abruptly to trouble about the Morlocks, and was only concerned in banishing these signs of human inheritance from Weena's eyes. And very soon she was smiling and clapping her hands while I solemnly burned a match.

---

1 **Utopian books** books which describe an imaginary perfect social and political system – 3 **supposition** guess – 7 **to dwindle** to become less and less – 12 **modification** change – 15 **troublesome** disturbing – 22 **to shiver** to tremble from cold or fear – 23 **unendurable** *here:* too terrible to talk about – 27 **inheritance** *here:* quality received from earlier generations

6

"It may seem odd to you, but it was two days before I could follow up the new-found clue in what was manifestly the proper way. I felt a peculiar shrinking from those pallid bodies. They
5 were just the half-bleached colour of the worms and things one sees preserved in spirit in a zoological museum. And they were filthily cold to the touch. Probably my shrinking was largely due to the sympathetic influence of the Eloi, whose disgust of the Morlocks I now began to appreciate.

10 "The next night I did not sleep well. Probably my health was a little disordered. I was oppressed with perplexity and doubt. Once or twice I had a feeling of intense fear for which I could perceive no definite reason. I remember creeping noiselessly into the great hall where the little people were sleeping in the
15 moonlight — that night Weena was among them — and feeling reassured by their presence. It occurred to me, even then, that in the course of a few days the moon must pass through its last quarter, and the nights grow dark, when the appearances of these unpleasant creatures from below, these whitened Lemurs,
20 this new vermin that had replaced the old, might be more abundant. And on both these days I had the restless feeling of one who shirks an inevitable duty. I felt assured that the Time Machine was only to be recovered by boldly penetrating these underground mysteries. Yet I could not face the mystery. If only
25 I had had a companion it would have been different. But I was so horribly alone, and even to clamber down into the darkness of the well appalled me. I don't know if you will understand my feeling, but I never felt quite safe at my back.

"It was this restlessness, this insecurity, perhaps, that drove
30 me further and further afield in my exploring expeditions. Going

---

3 **manifestly** plainly, obviously – 4 **to shrink (shrank, shrunk) from** to move back from, to show dislike for – 4 **pallid** pale, ill-looking – 6 **spirit** *here:* alcohol – 13 **definite** clear, specific – 20 **vermin** wild animals like rats which are harmful to other animals – 22 **to shirk** to avoid, to try to escape – 23 **to penetrate** to force a way into, to see into – 27 **to appal** [əˈpɔːl] to fill with fear – 30 **afield** away

to the south-westward towards the rising country that is now called Combe Wood, I observed far off, in the direction of nineteenth-century Banstead, a vast green structure, different in character from any I had hitherto seen. It was larger than the largest of the palaces or ruins I knew, and the facade had an Oriental look: the face of it having the lustre, as well as the pale-green tint, a kind of bluish-green, of a certain type of Chinese porcelain. This difference in aspect suggested a difference in use, and I was minded to push on and explore. But the day was growing late, and I had come upon the sight of the place after a long and tiring circuit; so I resolved to hold over the adventure for the following day, and I returned to the welcome and the caresses of little Weena. But next morning I perceived clearly enough that my curiosity regarding the Palace of Green Porcelain was a piece of self-deception, to enable me to shirk, by another day, an experience I dreaded. I resolved I would make the descent without further waste of time, and started out in the early morning towards a well near the ruins of granite and aluminium.

"Little Weena ran with me. She danced beside me to the well, but when she saw me lean over the mouth and look downward, she seemed strangely disconcerted. 'Good-bye, little Weena,' I said, kissing her; and then, putting her down, I began to feel over the parapet for the climbing hooks. Rather hastily, I may as well confess, for I feared my courage might leak away! At first she watched me in amazement. Then she gave a most piteous cry, and, running to me, she began to pull at me with her little hands. I think her opposition nerved me rather to proceed. I shook her off, perhaps a little roughly, and in another moment I was in the throat of the well. I saw her agonised face over the

6 **lustre** brightness of a shiny surface – 7 **tint** pale or delicate degree of colour – 9 **I was minded** *old use:* I wished – 11 **circuit** ['sɜːkɪt] *here:* journey or walk round the country – 11 **to hold over** to move to a later date – 22 **disconcerted** anxious and confused – 24 **hook** *here:* metal hold for hands and feet – 26 **piteous** causing or showing pity – 30 **throat** *here:* cylindrical opening

parapet, and smiled to reassure her. Then I had to look down at the unstable hooks to which I clung.

"I had to clamber down a shaft of perhaps two hundred yards.
The descent was effected by means of metallic bars projecting
5 from the sides of the well, and these being adapted to the needs of a creature much smaller and lighter than myself, I was speedily cramped and fatigued by the descent. And not simply fatigued! One of the bars bent suddenly under my weight, and almost swung me off into the blackness beneath. For a moment I hung
10 by one hand, and after that experience I did not dare to rest again. Though my arms and back were presently acutely painful, I went on clambering down the sheer descent with as quick a motion as possible. Glancing upward, I saw the aperture, a small blue disk, in which a star was visible, while little Weena's head
15 showed as a round black projection. The thudding sound of a machine below grew louder and more oppressive. Everything save that little disk above was profoundly dark, and when I looked up again Weena had disappeared.

"I was in an agony of discomfort. I had some thought of trying
20 to go up the shaft again, and leave the Underworld alone. But even while I turned this over in my mind I continued to descend. At last, with intense relief, I saw dimly coming up, a foot to the right of me, a slender loophole in the wall. Swinging myself in, I found it was the aperture of a narrow horizontal tunnel in
25 which I could lie down and rest. It was not too soon. My arms ached, my back was cramped, and I was trembling with the prolonged terror of a fall. Besides this, the unbroken darkness had had a distressing effect upon my eyes. The air was full of the throb and hum of machinery pumping air down the shaft.

30 "I do not know how long I lay. I was roused by a soft hand touching my face. Starting up in the darkness I snatched at my

2 **unstable** not firm – 9 **to swing (swung, swung) s.o. off** to cause s.o. to fall – 14 **disk** round area or surface – 19 **agony** ['ægənɪ] great pain of mind or body – 23 **slender** narrow – 23 **loophole** small opening in the wall – 25 **to ache** [eɪk] to suffer a steady pain – 28 **throb** beat – 29 **hum** steady low sound – 30 **to rouse** to cause s.o. to wake up or become active – 31 **to snatch** to take s.th. in a hurry

matches and, hastily striking one, I saw three stooping white
creatures similar to the one I had seen above ground in the ruin,
hastily retreating before the light. Living, as they did, in what
appeared to me impenetrable darkness, their eyes were
abnormally large and sensitive, just as are the pupils of the
abysmal fishes, and they reflected the light in the same way. I
have no doubt they could see me in that rayless obscurity, and
they did not seem to have any fear of me apart from the light.
But, so soon as I struck a match in order to see them, they fled
incontinently, vanishing into dark gutters and tunnels, from
which their eyes glared at me in the strangest fashion.

"I tried to call to them, but the language they had was
apparently different from that of the Over-world people; so that
I was needs left to my own unaided efforts, and the thought of
flight before exploration was even then in my mind. But I said
to myself, 'You are in for it now,' and, feeling my way along the
tunnel, I found the noise of machinery grow louder. Presently
the walls fell away from me, and I came to a large open space,
and, striking another match, saw that I had entered a vast arched
cavern, which stretched into utter darkness beyond the range
of my light. The view I had of it was as much as one could see
in the burning of a match.

"Necessarily my memory is vague. Great shapes like big
machines rose out of the dimness, and cast grotesque black
shadows, in which dim spectral Morlocks sheltered from the
glare. The place, by the bye, was very stuffy and oppressive, and
the faint halitus of freshly shed blood was in the air. Some way
down the central vista was a little table of white metal, laid with
what seemed a meal. The Morlocks at any rate were carnivorous!

1 **to stoop** to bend down – 5 **pupil** *here:* black opening in the middle of the eye –
6 **abysmal** *here:* living in deep waters – 7 **rayless** without light – 10 **gutter** small ditch,
normally to carry away rainwater – 14 **needs** *old use:* necessarily – 16 **You are in for it.**
There is definitely going to be trouble. – 25 **spectral** ghost-like – 26 **glare** strong light;
here: of the Time Traveller's burning match – 26 **stuffy** full of bad air – 27 **halitus** *med.*
bad smell – 27 **to shed, shed, shed** *lit.* to cause to flow – 28 **vista** view – 29 **carnivorous**
[-'---] flesh-eating

Even at the time, I remember wondering what large animal could have survived to furnish the red joint I saw. It was all very indistinct: the heavy smell, the big unmeaning shapes, the obscene figures lurking in the shadows, and only waiting for the
5   darkness to come at me again! Then the match burned down, and stung my fingers, and fell, a wriggling red spot in the blackness.

"I have thought since how particularly ill equipped I was for such an experience. When I had started with the Time Machine,
10 I had started with the absurd assumption that the men of the Future would certainly be infinitely ahead of ourselves in all their appliances. I had come without arms, without medicine, without anything to smoke — at times I missed tobacco frightfully! — even without enough matches. If only I had thought
15 of a Kodak! I could have flashed that glimpse of the Underworld in a second, and examined it at leisure. But, as it was, I stood there with only the weapons and the powers that Nature had endowed me with — hands, feet, and teeth; these, and four safety-matches that still remained to me.

20 "I was afraid to push my way in among all this machinery in the dark, and it was only with my last glimpse of light I discovered that my store of matches had run low. It had never occurred to me until that moment that there was any need to economise them, and I had wasted almost half the box in astonishing the
25 Upperworlders, to whom fire was a novelty. Now, as I say, I had four left, and while I stood in the dark, a hand touched mine, lank fingers came feeling over my face, and I was sensible of a peculiar unpleasant odour. I fancied I heard the breathing of a crowd of those dreadful little beings about me. I felt the box of
30 matches in my hand being gently disengaged, and other hands

---

2 **to furnish** *formal:* to supply – 2 **joint** large piece of meat for cooking – 4 **to lurk** to wait in hiding – 6 **to wriggle** to twist – 15 **to flash** *here:* to take a flash photograph – 16 **at leisure** without any hurry – 18 **to endow s.o. with s.th.** to provide s.o. with s.th. – 23 **to economise s.th.** to use s.th. without wasting it – 25 **novelty** s.th. new – 27 **lank** long and thin – 28 **odour** [ˈəʊdə] smell – 30 **to disengage** to pull away, to take away

behind me plucking at my clothing. The sense of these unseen creatures examining me was indescribably unpleasant. The sudden realisation of my ignorance of their ways of thinking and doing came home to me very vividly in the darkness. I shouted at them as loudly as I could. They started away, and then I could feel them approaching me again. They clutched at me more boldly, whispering odd sounds to each other. I shivered violently, and shouted again — rather discordantly. This time they were not so seriously alarmed, and they made a queer laughing noise as they came back at me. I will confess I was horribly frightened. I determined to strike another match and escape under the protection of its glare. I did so, and eking out the flicker with a scrap of paper from my pocket, I made good my retreat to the narrow tunnel. But I had scarce entered this when my light was blown out, and in the blackness I could hear the Morlocks rustling like wind among leaves, and pattering like the rain, as they hurried after me.

"In a moment I was clutched by several hands, and there was no mistaking that they were trying to haul me back. I struck another light, and waved it in their dazzled faces. You can scarce imagine how nauseatingly inhuman they looked — those pale, chinless faces and great, lidless, pinkish-grey eyes! — as they stared in their blindness and bewilderment. But I did not stay to look, I promise you: I retreated again, and when my second match had ended, I struck my third. It had almost burned through when I reached the opening into the shaft. I lay down on the edge, for the throb of the great pump below made me giddy. Then I felt sideways for the projecting hooks, and, as I did so, my feet were grasped from behind, and I was violently tugged

1 **to pluck** to take hold of and pull – 6 **to clutch at** to try to seize – 8 **discordant** loud and unpleasant, not harmonious – 13 **to make good** to be successful at doing s.th. – 16 **to patter** to make light rapidly repeated noises – 19 **to haul** to pull – 20 **dazzled** unable to see because of the light – 21 **nauseating** ['nɔːsɪeɪtɪŋ] making one feel sick – 23 **bewilderment** confusion – 27 **giddy** unsteady, feeling that one cannot stand firm – 29 **to tug** to pull

backward. I lit my last match … and it incontinently went out. But I had my hand on the climbing bars now, and, kicking violently, I disengaged myself from the clutches of the Morlocks, and was speedily clambering up the shaft, while they stayed
5 peering and blinking up at me: all but one little wretch who followed me for some way, and well-nigh secured my boot as a trophy.

"That climb seemed interminable to me. With the last twenty or thirty feet of it a deadly nausea came upon me. I had the
10 greatest difficulty in keeping my hold. The last few yards was a frightful struggle against this faintness. Several times my head swam, and I felt all the sensation of falling. At last, however, I got over the well-mouth somehow, and staggered out of the ruin into the blinding sunlight. I fell upon my face. Even the soil
15 smelt sweet and clean. Then I remember Weena kissing my hands and ears, and the voices of others among the Eloi. Then, for a time, I was insensible.

7

"Now, indeed, I seemed in a worse case than before. Hitherto,
20 except during my night's anguish at the loss of the Time Machine, I had felt a sustaining hope of ultimate escape, but that hope was staggered by these new discoveries. Hitherto I had merely thought myself impeded by the childish simplicity of the little people, and by some unknown forces which I had only to
25 understand to overcome; but there was an altogether new element in the sickening quality of the Morlocks — a something inhuman and malign. Instinctively I loathed them. Before, I had felt as a man might feel who had fallen into a pit: my concern

---

5 **to blink** to look, quickly shutting and opening one's eyes – 5 **wretch** mean little fellow – 6 **well-nigh** *formal:* almost – 7 **trophy** object taken in war as a souvenir of victory – 8 **interminable** endless – 9 **nausea** feeling of sickness – 17 **insensible** *formal:* unconscious – 21 **to sustain** to give strength – 21 **ultimate escape** escaping in the end – 23 **to impede** to make things difficult for – 27 **malign** [mə'laɪn] *lit.* evil, harmful – 27 **to loathe** [ləʊð] to hate, to dislike very much

was with the pit and how to get out of it. Now I felt like a beast in a trap, whose enemy would come upon him soon.

"The enemy I dreaded may surprise you. It was the darkness of the new moon. Weena had put this into my head by some at
5 first incomprehensible remarks about the Dark Nights. It was not now such a very difficult problem to guess what the coming Dark Nights might mean. The moon was on the wane: each night there was a longer interval of darkness. And I now understood to some slight degree at least the reason of the fear of the little
10 Upperworld people for the dark. I wondered vaguely what foul villainy it might be that the Morlocks did under the new moon. I felt pretty sure now that my second hypothesis was all wrong. The Upperworld people might once have been the favoured aristocracy, and the Morlocks their mechanical servants; but
15 that had long since passed away. The two species that had resulted from the evolution of man were sliding down towards, or had already arrived at, an altogether new relationship. The Eloi, like the Carlovingian kings, had decayed to a mere beautiful futility. They still possessed the earth on sufferance: since the
20 Morlocks, subterranean for innumerable generations, had come at last to find the daylit surface intolerable. And the Morlocks made their garments, I inferred, and maintained them in their habitual needs, perhaps through the survival of an old habit of service. They did it as a standing horse paws with his foot, or as
25 a man enjoys killing animals in sport: because ancient and departed necessities had impressed it on the organism. But, clearly, the old order was already in part reversed. The Nemesis of the delicate ones was creeping on apace. Ages ago, thousands of generations ago, man had thrust his brother man out of

5 **incomprehensible** not to be understood – 7 **on the wane** becoming smaller –
11 **villainy** ['vɪlənɪ] *lit.* evil behaviour – 18 **Carlovingian** referring to Charlemagne
(Charles the Great) and his successors – 19 **futility** uselessness – 19 **on sufferance** only
because the Morlocks had no objections – 22 **to infer** to draw the conclusion – 22 **to
maintain** to support, to keep up – 24 **to paw** *here:* to strike the ground with a
hoof – 26 **departed** no longer existent – 27 **Nemesis** just and unavoidable
punishment – 28 **apace** *lit., old use:* quickly – 29 **to thrust, thrust, thrust** to push
forcefully

the ease and the sunshine. And now that brother was coming back — changed! Already the Eloi had begun to learn one old lesson anew. They were becoming reacquainted with Fear. And suddenly there came into my head the memory of the meat I
5 had seen in the Underworld. It seemed odd how it floated into my mind: not stirred up as it were by the current of my meditations, but coming in almost like a question from outside. I tried to recall the form of it. I had a vague sense of something familiar, but I could not tell what it was at the time.

10 "Still, however helpless the little people in the presence of their mysterious Fear, I was differently constituted. I came out of this age of ours, this ripe prime of the human race, when Fear does not paralyse and mystery has lost its terrors. I at least would defend myself. Without further delay I determined to make
15 myself arms and a fastness where I might sleep. With that refuge as a base, I could face this strange world with some of that confidence I had lost in realising to what creatures night by night I lay exposed. I felt I could never sleep again until my bed was secure from them. I shuddered with horror to think how they
20 must already have examined me.

"1 wandered during the afternoon along the valley of the Thames, but found nothing that commended itself to my mind as inaccessible. All the buildings and trees seemed easily practicable to such dexterous climbers as the Morlocks, to judge
25 by their wells, must be. Then the tall pinnacles of the Palace of Green Porcelain and the polished gleam of its walls came back to my memory; and in the evening, taking Weena like a child upon my shoulder, I went up the hills towards the south-west. The distance, I had reckoned, was seven or eight miles, but it

---

3 **to become reacquainted with** to learn about again – 8 **to recall** to remember –
12 **prime** time of greatest strength and activity – 13 **to paralyse** to make s.o. unable to move or act – 15 **fastness** a safe place which is hard to reach or enter – 15 **refuge** ['refju:dʒ] safe place to which one can escape – 22 **to commend o.s.** *formal:* to appear to be useful or attractive – 23 **inaccessible** difficult to reach or enter – 24 **practicable** accessible – 24 **dexterous** skilful – 25 **pinnacle** tower-like stone ornament on the roof of an old church or castle

must have been nearer eighteen. I had first seen the place on a moist afternoon when distances are deceptively diminished. In addition, the heel of one of my shoes was loose, and a nail was working through the sole — they were comfortable old shoes I
5   wore about indoors — so that I was lame. And it was already long past sunset when I came in sight of the palace, silhouetted black against the pale yellow of the sky.

"Weena had been hugely delighted when I began to carry her, but after a time she desired me to let her down, and ran along
10 by the side of me, occasionally darting off on either hand to pick flowers to stick in my pockets. My pockets had always puzzled Weena, but at the last she had concluded that they were an eccentric kind of vase for floral decoration. At least she utilised them for that purpose. And that reminds me! In changing my
15 jacket I found …"

The Time Traveller paused, put his hand into his pocket, and silently placed two withered flowers, not unlike very large white mallows, upon the little table. Then he resumed his narrative.

"As the hush of evening crept over the world and we proceeded
20 over the hill crest towards Wimbledon, Weena grew tired and wanted to return to the house of grey stone. But I pointed out the distant pinnacles of the Palace of Green Porcelain to her, and contrived to make her understand that we were seeking a refuge there from her Fear. You know that great pause that comes
25 upon things before the dusk? Even the breeze stops in the trees. To me there is always an air of expectation about that evening stillness. The sky was clear, remote, and empty save for a few horizontal bars far down in the sunset. Well, that night the expectation took the colour of my fears. In that darkling calm
30 my senses seemed preternaturally sharpened. I fancied I could

---

2 **moist** rainy – 2 **to diminish** to make smaller – 12 **to conclude** to come to believe –
17 **withered** dry and faded – 18 **mallow** plant with hairy stems and leaves and pink,
mauve or white flowers – 18 **narrative** story – 19 **hush** silence, quiet – 23 **to contrive** to
find a way, to manage – 25 **breeze** light wind – 30 **preternatural** [ˌpriːtəˈnætʃrəl]
beyond what is natural

even feel the hollowness of the ground beneath my feet: could, indeed, almost see through it the Morlocks in their anthill going hither and thither and waiting for the dark. In my excitement I fancied that they would receive my invasion of their burrows
5 as a declaration of war. And why had they taken my Time Machine?

"So we went on in the quiet, and the twilight deepened into night. The clear blue of the distance faded, and one star after another came out. The ground grew dim and the trees black.
10 Weena's fears and her fatigue grew upon her. I took her in my arms and talked to her and caressed her. Then, as the darkness grew deeper, she put her arms round my neck, and, closing her eyes, tightly pressed her face against my shoulder. So we went down a long slope into a valley, and there in the dimness I almost
15 walked into a little river. This I waded, and went up the opposite side of the valley, past a number of sleeping houses, and by a statue — a Faun, or some such figure, *minus* the head. Here too were acacias. So far I had seen nothing of the Morlocks, but it was yet early in the night, and the darker hours before the old
20 moon rose were still to come.

"From the brow of the next hill I saw a thick wood spreading wide and black before me. I hesitated at this. I could see no end to it, either to the right or the left. Feeling tired — my feet in particular, were very sore — I carefully lowered Weena from my
25 shoulder as I halted, and sat down upon the turf. I could no longer see the Palace of Green Porcelain, and I was in doubt of my direction. I looked into the thickness of the wood and thought of what it might hide. Under that dense tangle of branches one would be out of sight of the stars. Even were there no other
30 lurking danger — a danger I did not care to let my imagination

2 **anthill** small hill constructed by ants – 4 **burrow** hole in the ground in which an animal lives – 17 **Faun** Roman god of the fields and woods, believed to look like a man with a goat's horns and legs – 17 **minus** without – 18 **acacia** [ə'keɪʃə] tree grown as an ornament in parks – 21 **brow** *here:* upper part of a hill – 28 **tangle** confused mass

loose upon — there would still be all the roots to stumble over and the tree-boles to strike against. I was very tired, too, after the excitements of the day; so I decided that I would not face it, but would pass the night upon the open hill.

5 "Weena, I was glad to find, was fast asleep. I carefully wrapped her in my jacket, and sat down beside her to wait for the moonrise. The hillside was quiet and deserted, but from the black of the wood there came now and then a stir of living things. Above me shone the stars, for the night was very clear. I felt a

10 certain sense of friendly comfort in their twinkling. All the old constellations had gone from the sky, however: that slow movement which is imperceptible in a hundred human lifetimes, had long since rearranged them in unfamiliar groupings. But the Milky Way, it seemed to me, was still the same tattered streamer

15 of star-dust as of yore. Southward (as I judged it) was a very bright red star that was new to me; it was even more splendid than our own green Sirius. And amid all these scintillating points of light one bright planet shone kindly and steadily like the face of an old friend.

20 "Looking at these stars suddenly dwarfed my own troubles and all the gravities of terrestrial life. I thought of their unfathomable distance, and the slow inevitable drift of their movements out of the unknown past into the unknown future. I thought of the great precessional cycle that the pole of the

25 earth describes. Only forty times had that silent revolution occurred during all the years that I had traversed. And during these few revolutions all the activity, all the traditions, the

---

2 **tree-bole** tree-trunk – 12 **imperceptible** so slight that it cannot be noticed – 14 **Milky Way** broad band of stars that can be seen across the sky at night – 14 **streamer** s.th. long and narrow like a flag – 15 **of yore** *lit.* in times long past – 17 **to scintillate** to send out small flashes of light – 20 **to dwarf** to make s.th. appear very small by comparison – 21 **gravities** worries – 21 **terrestrial** on earth – 22 **unfathomable** immense, which cannot be measured – 24 **precessional cycle** an extremely slow circular movement of the earth's axis, which causes the times of the year at which day and night are both exactly 12 hours long to be slightly earlier each year – 25 **revolution** *here:* circular movement

complex organisations, the nations, languages, literatures, aspirations, even the mere memory of Man as I knew him, had been swept out of existence. Instead were these frail creatures who had forgotten their high ancestry, and the white Things of
5 which I went in terror. Then I thought of the Great Fear that was between the two species, and for the first time, with a sudden shiver, came the clear knowledge of what the meat I had seen might be. Yet it was too horrible! I looked at little Weena sleeping beside me, her face white and starlike under the stars, and
10 forthwith dismissed the thought.

"Through that long night I held my mind off the Morlocks as well as I could, and whiled away the time by trying to fancy I could find signs of the old constellations in the new confusion. The sky kept very clear, except for a hazy cloud or so. No doubt
15 I dozed at times. Then, as my vigil wore on, came a faintness in the eastward sky, like the reflection of some colourless fire, and the old moon rose, thin and peaked and white. And close behind, and overtaking it, and overflowing it, the dawn came, pale at first, and then growing pink and warm. No Morlocks had
20 approached us. Indeed, I had seen none upon the hill that night. And in the confidence of renewed day it almost seemed to me that my fear had been unreasonable. I stood up and found my foot with the loose heel swollen at the ankle and painful under the heel; so I sat down again, took off my shoes, and flung them
25 away.

"I awakened Weena, and we went down into the wood, now green and pleasant instead of black and forbidding. We found some fruit wherewith to break our fast. We soon met others of the dainty ones, laughing and dancing in the sunlight as though
30 there was no such thing in nature as the night. And then I thought once more of the meat that I had seen. I felt assured now of

---

4 **ancestry** persons living a long time ago, from whom s.o. is descended – 12 **to while away the time** to pass the time in a lazy or pleasant manner – 14 **hazy** of thin mist – 15 **to doze** to sleep lightly – 23 **to swell, swelled, swollen** to become thick and round, to become larger than usual – 28 **wherewith to break our fast** *old use:* with which to have breakfast – 29 **dainty** pretty and delicate

what it was, and from the bottom of my heart I pitied this last feeble rill from the great flood of humanity. Clearly, at some time in the Long-Ago of human decay the Morlocks' food had run short. Possibly they had lived on rats and suchlike vermin. Even now man is far less discriminating and exclusive in his food than he was — far less than any monkey. His prejudice against human flesh is no deep-seated instinct. And so these inhuman sons of men —! I tried to look at the thing in a scientific spirit. After all, they were less human and more remote than our cannibal ancestors of three or four thousand years ago. And the intelligence that would have made this state of things a torment had gone. Why should I trouble myself? These Eloi were mere fatted cattle, which the ant-like Morlocks preserved and preyed upon — probably saw to the breeding of. And there was Weena dancing at my side!

"Then I tried to preserve myself from the horror that was coming upon me, by regarding it as a rigorous punishment of human selfishness. Man had been content to live in ease and delight upon the labours of his fellow man, had taken Necessity as his watchword and excuse, and in the fullness of time Necessity had come home to him. I even tried a Carlyle-like scorn of this wretched aristocracy in decay. But this attitude of mind was impossible. However great their intellectual degradation, the Eloi had kept too much of the human form not to claim my sympathy, and to make me perforce a sharer in their degradation and their Fear.

"I had at that time very vague ideas as to the course I should pursue. My first was to secure some safe place of refuge, and to make myself such arms of metal or stone as I could contrive.

---

2 **feeble** weak, faint – 2 **rill** *poet., here fig.* small stream – 5 **discriminating** able to choose what is best – 13 **fatted** fattened for eating – 13 **to prey upon** to hunt and eat – 20 **watchword** word that expresses a guiding principle – 20 **in the fullness of time** *lit.* when the right time came – 21 **Carlyle, Thomas** (1795–1881) Scottish writer and historian – 22 **scorn** feeling of disrespect – 24 **degradation** decadence, less deserving of respect – 25 **perforce** *old use:* necessarily – 27 **as to** with regard to

That necessity was immediate. In the next place, I hoped to procure some means of fire, so that I should have the weapon of a torch at hand, for nothing, I knew, would be more efficient against these Morlocks. Then I wanted to arrange some contrivance to break open the doors of bronze under the White Sphinx. I had in mind a battering-ram. I had a persuasion that if I could enter those doors and carry a blaze of light before me I should discover the Time Machine and escape. I could not imagine the Morlocks were strong enough to move it far away. Weena I had resolved to bring with me to our own time. And turning such schemes over in my mind I pursued our way towards the building which my fancy had chosen as our dwelling.

8

"I found the Palace of Green Porcelain, when we approached it about noon, deserted and falling into ruin. Only ragged vestiges of glass remained in its windows, and great sheets of the green facing had fallen away from the corroded metallic framework. It lay very high upon a turfy down, and looking north-eastward before I entered it, I was surprised to see a large estuary, or even creek, where I judged Wandsworth and Battersea must once have been. I thought then — though I never followed up the thought — of what might have happened, or might be happening, to the living things in the sea.

"The material of the Palace proved on examination to be indeed porcelain, and along the face of it I saw an inscription in some unknown character. I thought, rather foolishly, that

---

2 **to procure** to obtain – 3 **torch** burning piece of wood or other material, carried to give light – 5 **contrivance** device – 6 **battering-ram** (in former times) a tree-trunk with an iron end, used for breaking through the gates and walls of castles and towns – 15 **ragged** *here:* with broken, uneven edges – 17 **facing** outer covering or surface of a wall – 17 **corroded** worn, partly destroyed by chemical action or the weather – 18 **down** open hilly land in Southern England – 19 **estuary** river mouth – 20 **creek** long, narrow stretch of water reaching from the sea into the land – 20 **Wandsworth and Battersea** two parts of London situated south of the Thames – 26 **character** *here:* letters, writing

Weena might help me to interpret this, but I only learned that the bare idea of writing had never entered her head. She always seemed to me, I fancy, more human than she was, perhaps because her affection was so human.

5   "Within the big valves of the door — which were open and broken — we found, instead of the customary hall, a long gallery lit by many side windows. At the first glance I was reminded of a museum. The tiled floor was thick with dust, and a remarkable array of miscellaneous objects was shrouded in the same grey
10 covering. Then I perceived, standing strange and gaunt in the centre of the hall, what was clearly the lower part of a huge skeleton. I recognised by the oblique feet that it was some extinct creature after the fashion of the Megatherium. The skull and the upper bones lay beside it in the thick dust, and in one place,
15 where rain-water had dropped through a leak in the roof, the thing itself had been worn away. Further in the gallery was the huge skeleton barrel of a Brontosaurus. My museum hypothesis was confirmed. Going towards the side I found what appeared to be sloping shelves, and, clearing away the thick dust, I found
20 the old familiar glass cases of our own time. But they must have been air-tight, to judge from the fair preservation of some of their contents.

    "Clearly we stood among the ruins of some latter-day South Kensington! Here, apparently, was the Palaeontological Section,
25 and a very splendid array of fossils it must have been, though

---

4 **affection** gentle love – 5 **valve** *here, obs.* one half of a double door – 6 **customary** usual – 8 **tiled** covered with plates of baked clay – 9 **array** collection – 9 **miscellaneous** [ˌmɪsəˈleɪnɪes] of different kinds – 9 **shrouded** covered and hidden – 10 **gaunt** very thin – 12 **skeleton** framework of a body, made up of bones – 12 **oblique** [əˈbliːk] sloping, at an angle – 12 **extinct** no longer in existence – 13 **after the fashion** of similar to – 13 **megatherium** [ˌmegəˈθiːrɪəm] huge slow-moving prehistoric animal – 13 **skull** the bone of the head – 17 **brontosaurus** [ˌbrɒntəˈsɔːrəs] a kind of dinosaur – 18 **to be confirmed** to prove true – 23 **latter-day** recent, modern – 23 **South Kensington** *here:* the Natural History and Science Museums of South Kensington in London – 24 **Palaeontological Section** the part of the museum concerned with fossils – 25 **fossil** hardened part of an animal or plant of long ago that has been preserved by rock

85

the inevitable process of decay that had been staved off for a time, and had, through the extinction of bacteria and fungi, lost ninety-nine hundredths of its force, was, nevertheless, with extreme sureness if with extreme slowness at work again upon all its treasures. Here and there I found traces of the little people in the shape of rare fossils broken to pieces or threaded in strings upon reeds. And the cases had in some instances been bodily removed — by the Morlocks as I judged. The place was very silent. The thick dust deadened our footsteps. Weena, who had been rolling a sea-urchin down the sloping glass of a case, presently came, as I stared about me, and very quietly took my hand and stood beside me.

"And at first I was so much surprised by this ancient monument of an intellectual age, that I gave no thought to the possibilities it presented. Even my preoccupation about the Time Machine receded a little from my mind.

"To judge from the size of the place, this Palace of Green Porcelain had a great deal more in it than a Gallery of Palaeontology; possibly historical galleries; it might be, even a library! To me, at least in my present circumstances, these would be vastly more interesting than this spectacle of old-time geology in decay. Exploring, I found another short gallery running transversely to the first. This appeared to be devoted to minerals, and the sight of a block of sulphur set my mind running on gunpowder. But I could find no saltpetre; indeed, no nitrates of any kind. Doubtless they had deliquesced ages ago. Yet the sulphur hung in my mind, and set up a train of thinking. As for the rest of the contents of that gallery, though on the whole they

---

1 **to stave off** to keep away, to delay – 2 **fungus** *pl.* **fungi** a simple type of plant growing on decaying matter – 6 **to thread** to connect by running s.th. through – 6 **in strings** one after the other in a line – 7 **reed** a tall grasslike plant that grows in wet places – 7 **bodily** as a whole, completely – 10 **sea-urchin** small ball-shaped sea animal with many sharp points – 15 **preoccupation** concern – 16 **to recede** to move away, to become less – 23 **transversely** at right angles – 23 **to devote to** to intend for – 24 **sulphur** a light-yellow chemical element (S) – 25 **saltpetre** a salty white powder used for making gunpowder – 26 **to deliquesce** [ˌdelɪˈkwes] *tech.* to take up water from the air and become liquid

were the best preserved of all I saw, I had little interest. I am no specialist in mineralogy, and I went on down a very ruinous aisle running parallel to the first hall I had entered. Apparently this section had been devoted to natural history, but everything had long since passed out of recognition. A few shrivelled and blackened vestiges of what had once been stuffed animals, desiccated mummies in jars that had once held spirit, a brown dust of departed plants; that was all! I was sorry for that, because I should have been glad to trace the patient readjustments by which the conquest of animated nature had been attained. Then we came to a gallery of simply colossal proportions, but singularly ill-lit, the floor of it running downward at a slight angle from the end at which I entered. At intervals white globes hung from the ceiling — many of them cracked and smashed — which suggested that originally the place had been artificially lit. Here I was more in my element, for rising on either side of me were the huge bulks of big machines, all greatly corroded and many broken down, but some still fairly complete. You know I have a certain weakness for mechanism, and I was inclined to linger among these; the more so as for the most part they had the interest of puzzles, and I could make only the vaguest guesses at what they were for. I fancied that if I could solve their puzzles I should find myself in possession of powers that might be of use against the Morlocks.

"Suddenly Weena came very close to my side. So suddenly that she startled me. Had it not been for her I do not think I should have noticed that the floor of the gallery sloped at all.*

* It may be, of course, that the floor did not slope, but that the museum was built into the side of a hill. — Ed.

2 **aisle** [aɪl] passage – 5 **out of recognition** so that it could no longer be recognized – 5 **to shrivel** to dry out and become smaller – 6 **to stuff** to fill the skin of a dead animal – 7 **to desiccate** to dry out completely – 7 **mummy** dead body preserved from decay – 9 **readjustment** change in order to become suitable for new conditions – 13 **globe** *here:* ball-like cover for a lamp – 17 **bulk** big shape or mass – 19 **to be inclined to** to feel a wish to – 20 **to linger** to stay at a place for a while

The end I had come in at was quite above ground, and was lit by rare slit-like windows. As you went down the length, the ground came up against these windows, until at last there was a pit like the 'area' of a London house before each, and only a narrow line of daylight at the top. I went slowly along, puzzling about the machines, and had been too intent upon them to notice the gradual diminution of the light, until Weena's increasing apprehensions drew my attention. Then I saw that the gallery ran down at last into a thick darkness. I hesitated, and then, as I looked round me, I saw that the dust was less abundant and its surface less even. Further away towards the dimness, it appeared to be broken by a number of small narrow footprints. My sense of the immediate presence of the Morlocks revived at that. I felt that I was wasting my time in this academic examination of machinery. I called to mind that it was already far advanced in the afternoon, and that I had still no weapon, no refuge, and no means of making a fire. And then down in the remote blackness of the gallery I heard a peculiar pattering, and the same odd noises I had heard down the well.

"I took Weena's hand. Then, struck with a sudden idea, I left her and turned to a machine from which projected a lever not unlike those in a signal-box. Clambering upon the stand, and grasping this lever in my hands, I put all my weight upon it sideways. Suddenly Weena, deserted in the central aisle, began to whimper. I had judged the strength of the lever pretty correctly, for it snapped after a minute's strain, and I rejoined her with a mace in my hand more than sufficient, I judged, for any Morlock skull I might encounter. And I longed very much to kill a Morlock

2 **slit-like** very narrow – 4 **the 'area'** a space outside the lowest row of windows which is only a few metres wide and well below street-level – 7 **diminution** becoming less and less – 8 **apprehensions** anxiety – 14 **to revive** to become strong again – 21 **to project** [-'-] to stand out – 22 **signal-box** small building near a railway from which traffic on the line is controlled – 22 **stand** small stage – 25 **to whimper** to make weak cries of fear – 26 **to snap** to break suddenly – 26 **strain** effort – 27 **mace** short heavy stick or club used as a weapon – 28 **to encounter** to meet

or so. Very inhuman, you may think, to want to go killing one's own descendants! But it was impossible, somehow, to feel any humanity in the things. Only my disinclination to leave Weena, and a persuasion that if I began to slake my thirst for murder
5 my Time Machine might suffer, restrained me from going straight down the gallery and killing the brutes I heard.

"Well, mace in one hand and Weena in the other, I went out of that gallery and into another and still larger one, which at the first glance reminded me of a military chapel hung with tattered
10 flags. The brown and charred rags that hung from the sides of it, I presently recognised as the decaying vestiges of books. They had long since dropped to pieces, and every semblance of print had left them. But here and there were warped boards and cracked metallic clasps that told the tale well enough. Had I
15 been a literary man I might, perhaps, have moralised upon the futility of all ambition. But as it was, the thing that struck me with keenest force was the enormous waste of labour to which this sombre wilderness of rotting paper testified. At the time I will confess that I thought chiefly of the *Philosophical*
20 *Transactions* and my own seventeen papers upon physical optics.

"Then, going up a broad staircase, we came to what may once have been a gallery of technical chemistry. And here I had not a little hope of useful discoveries. Except at one end where the
25 roof had collapsed, this gallery was well preserved. I went eagerly to every unbroken case. And at last, in one of the really air-tight cases, I found a box of matches. Very eagerly I tried them. They

---

3 **disinclination** unwillingness – 4 **to slake** to satisfy – 5 **to restrain** to prevent, to hold back – 6 **brute** animal or animal-like person – 9 **chapel** small church or room in a church – 10 **charred** become black by burning – 10 **rag** old and torn piece of cloth – 12 **semblance** likeness – 13 **warped** twisted out of shape – 13 **board** *here:* cardboard used for the covers of books – 14 **clasp** piece of metal used for holding things together – 18 **to rot** to decay – 18 **to testify to s.th.** to bear witness to s.th. – 19 **Philosophical Transactions** a series of books on all fields of knowledge published by the Royal Society in London since 1665 – 20 **physical optics** the scientific study of light

were perfectly good. They were not even damp. I turned to Weena. 'Dance' I cried to her in her own tongue. For now I had a weapon indeed against the horrible creatures we feared. And so, in that derelict museum, upon the thick soft carpeting of
5 dust, to Weena's huge delight, I solemnly performed a kind of composite dance, whistling *The Land of the Leal* as cheerfully as I could. In part it was a modest *cancan*, in part a step-dance, in part a skirt-dance (so far as my tailcoat permitted), and in part original. For I am naturally inventive, as you know.

10   "Now, I still think that for this box of matches to have escaped the wear of time for immemorial years was a most strange, as for me it was a most fortunate thing. Yet, oddly enough, I found a far unlikelier substance, and that was camphor. I found it in a sealed jar, that by chance, I suppose, had been really
15 hermetically sealed. I fancied at first that it was paraffin wax, and smashed the glass accordingly. But the odour of camphor was unmistakable. In the universal decay this volatile substance had chanced to survive, perhaps through many thousands of centuries. It reminded me of a sepia painting I had once seen
20 done from the ink of a fossil Belemnite that must have perished and become fossilised millions of years ago. I was about to throw it away, but I remembered that it was inflammable and burned with a good bright flame — was, in fact, an excellent candle — and I put it in my pocket. I found no explosives, however, nor
25 any means of breaking down the bronze doors. As yet my iron crowbar was the most helpful thing I had chanced upon. Nevertheless I left that gallery greatly elated.

---

1 **damp** slightly wet – 4 **derelict** deserted, left to decay – 6 **leal** *Scottish:* loyal, true; **The Land of the Leal** the kingdom of the blessed souls, heaven – 8 **skirt-dance** a form of dancing in which the steps are accompanied by manipulating long flowing skirts – 8 **tailcoat** a man's formal evening coat with long divided back – 11 **immemorial** beyond the reach of memory – 13 **camphor** strong-smelling white substance used medically – 14 **to seal** to close with a tight cover – 15 **hermetical** air-tight – 17 **volatile** easily changing into gas – 19 **sepia** brown (ink or paint) – 20 **belemnite** extinct animal related to the cuttlefish – 26 **crowbar** iron bar used for breaking open things – 27 **elated** filled with joy

"I cannot tell you all the story of that long afternoon. It would require a great effort of memory to recall my explorations in at all the proper order. I remember a long gallery of rusting stands of arms, and how I hesitated between my crowbar and a hatchet
5   or a sword. I could not carry both, however, and my bar of iron promised best against the bronze gates. There were numbers of guns, pistols, and rifles. The most were masses of rust, but many were of some new metal, and still fairly sound. But any cartridges or powder there may once have been had rotted into dust. One
10   corner I saw was charred and shattered; perhaps, I thought, by an explosion among the specimens. In another place was a vast array of idols — Polynesian, Mexican, Grecian, Phoenician, every country on earth I should think. And here, yielding to an irresistible impulse, I wrote my name upon the nose of a steatite
15   monster from South America that particularly took my fancy.

"As the evening drew on, my interest waned. I went through gallery after gallery, dusty, silent, often ruinous, the exhibits sometimes mere heaps of rust and lignite, sometimes fresher. In one place I suddenly found myself near the model of a tin-
20   mine, and then by the merest accident I discovered, in an air-tight case, two dynamite cartridges! I shouted 'Eureka' and smashed the case with joy. Then came a doubt. I hesitated. Then, selecting a little side gallery, I made my essay. I never felt such a disappointment as I did in waiting five, ten, fifteen minutes
25   for an explosion that never came. Of course the things were dummies, as I might have guessed from their presence. I really believe that, had they not been so, I should have rushed off incontinently and blown sphinx, bronze doors, and (as it proved) my chances of finding the Time Machine, all together into non-
30   existence.

---

3 **stand of arms** weapons displayed on a stand – 4 **hatchet** axe – 8 **cartridge** metal tube containing explosive and a bullet – 10 **to shatter** to break into small pieces – 14 **steatite** of soapstone – 15 **to take s.o.'s fancy** to attract or please s.o. – 18 **lignite** coal-like material – 19 **tin-mine** place under the ground where tin, a soft white metal (Sn), is dug – 21 **Eureka** [juə'riːkə] *Greek:* I have found it! – 23 **essay** *formal:* attempt (*here:* to explode the cartridge) – 26 **dummy** object made to look like the real thing – 28 **to blow** *here:* to explode

"It was after that, I think, that we came to a little open court within the palace. It was turfed, and had three fruit-trees. So we rested and refreshed ourselves. Towards sunset I began to consider our position. Night was creeping upon us, and my
5 inaccessible hiding-place had still to be found. But that troubled me very little now. I had in my possession a thing that was, perhaps, the best of all defences against the Morlocks — I had matches! I had the camphor in my pocket, too, if a blaze were needed. It seemed to me that the best thing we could do would
10 be to pass the night in the open, protected by a fire. In the morning there was the getting of the Time Machine. Towards that, as yet, I had only my iron mace. But now, with my growing knowledge, I felt very differently towards those bronze doors. Up to this, I had refrained from forcing them, largely because of the
15 mystery on the other side. They had never impressed me as being very strong, and I hoped to find my bar of iron not altogether inadequate for the work.

9

"We emerged from the palace while the sun was still in part
20 above the horizon. I was determined to reach the White Sphinx early the next morning, and ere the dusk I purposed pushing through the woods that had stopped me on the previous journey. My plan was to go as far as possible that night, and then, building a fire, to sleep in the protection of its glare. Accordingly, as we
25 went along I gathered any sticks or dried grass I saw, and presently had my arms full of such litter. Thus loaded, our progress was slower than I had anticipated, and besides Weena was tired. And I began to suffer from sleepiness too; so that it was full night before we reached the wood. Upon the shrubby

---

11 **towards that** for that purpose – 12 **as yet** until now, so far – 13 **up to this** until this moment – 14 **to refrain to** hold o.s. back – 21 **ere** *poet., old use:* before – 26 **litter** *here:* pieces of various things – 29 **shrubby** covered with low bushes

hill of its edge Weena would have stopped, fearing the darkness before us; but a singular sense of impending calamity, that should indeed have served me as a warning, drove me onward. I had been without sleep for a night and two days, and I was feverish and irritable. I felt sleep coming upon me, and the Morlocks with it.

"While we hesitated, among the black bushes behind us, and dim against their blackness, I saw three crouching figures. There was scrub and long grass all about us, and I did not feel safe from their insidious approach. The forest, I calculated, was rather less than a mile across. If we could get through it to the bare hillside, there, as it seemed to me, was an altogether safer resting-place; I thought that with my matches and my camphor I could contrive to keep my path illuminated through the woods. Yet it was evident that if I was to flourish matches with my hands I should have to abandon my firewood; so, rather reluctantly, I put it down. And then it came into my head that I would amaze our friends behind by lighting it. I was to discover the atrocious folly of this proceeding, but it came to my mind as an ingenious move for covering our retreat.

"I don't know if you have ever thought what a rare thing flame must be in the absence of man and in a temperate climate. The sun's heat is rarely strong enough to burn, even when it is focussed by dewdrops, as is sometimes the case in more tropical districts. Lightning may blast and blacken, but it rarely gives rise to widespread fire. Decaying vegetation may occasionally smoulder with the heat of its fermentation, but this rarely results

---

2 **impending** about to happen, threatening – 2 **calamity** terrible event, disaster –
5 **irritable** easily made angry – 8 **to crouch** to lower the body with the arms and legs together, to hide close to the ground – 10 **insidious** secretly threatening – 14 **to contrive to** to succeed in – 15 **to flourish** to wave – 18 **atrocious** shocking – 19 **folly** stupidity – 22 **temperate** free from extremely high or low temperatures – 24 **to focus** to concentrate as if by a lens – 24 **dewdrop** small drop of water which forms on a cold surface during the night – 27 **to smoulder** to burn slowly without a flame –
27 **fermentation** chemical changes caused by organic bodies

in flame. In this decadence, too, the art of fire-making had been forgotten on the earth. The red tongues that went licking up my heap of wood were an altogether new and strange thing to Weena.

5 "She wanted to run to it and play with it. I believe she would have cast herself into it had I not restrained her. But I caught her up, and, in spite of her struggles, plunged before me into the wood. For a little way the glare of my fire lit the path. Looking back presently, I could see, through the crowded stems, that

10 from my heap of sticks the blaze had spread to some bushes adjacent, and a curved line of fire was creeping up the grass of the hill. I laughed at that, and turned again to the dark trees before me. It was very black, and Weena clung to me convulsively, but there was still, as my eyes grew accustomed to the darkness,

15 sufficient light for me to avoid the stems. Overhead it was simply black, except where a gap of remote blue sky shone down upon us here and there. I struck none of my matches because I had no hand free. Upon my left arm I carried my little one, in my right hand I had my iron bar.

20 "For some way I heard nothing but the crackling twigs under my feet, the faint rustle of the breeze above, and my own breathing and the throb of the blood-vessels in my ears. Then I seemed to know of a pattering about me. I pushed on grimly. The pattering grew more distinct, and then I caught the same

25 queer sounds and voices I had heard in the Underworld. There were evidently several of the Morlocks, and they were closing in upon me. Indeed, in another minute I felt a tug at my coat, then something at my arm. And Weena shivered violently, and became quite still.

---

2 **to lick** *here:* to move lightly like little tongues – 7 **to plunge** to move suddenly forwards – 9 **stem** tree-trunk – 11 **adjacent** very close, next (to the heap) – 13 **convulsively** with unnaturally violent movements – 21 **rustle** slight sound (like dry leaves moving in the wind) – 21 **breeze** light gentle wind – 23 **grim** *here:* determined in spite of fear – 26 **to close in upon s.o.** to come nearer, ready to attack

"It was time for a match. But to get one I must put her down. I did so, and, as I fumbled with my pocket, a struggle began in the darkness about my knees, perfectly silent on her part and with the same peculiar cooing sounds from the Morlocks. Soft little hands, too, were creeping over my coat and back, touching even my neck. Then the match scratched and fizzed. I held it flaring, and saw the white backs of the Morlocks in flight amid the trees. I hastily took a lump of camphor from my pocket, and prepared to light it as soon as the match should wane. Then I looked at Weena. She was lying clutching my feet and quite motionless, with her face to the ground. With a sudden fright I stooped to her. She seemed scarcely to breathe. I lit the block of camphor and flung it to the ground, and as it split and flared up and drove back the Morlocks and the shadows, I knelt down and lifted her. The wood behind seemed full of the stir and murmur of a great company!

"She seemed to have fainted. I put her carefully upon my shoulder and rose to push on, and then there came a horrible realisation. In manoeuvring with my matches and Weena, I had turned myself about several times, and now I had not the faintest idea in what direction lay my path. For all I knew, I might be facing back towards the Palace of Green Porcelain. I found myself in a cold sweat. I had to think rapidly what to do. I determined to build a fire and encamp where we were. I put Weena, still motionless, down upon a turfy bole, and very hastily, as my first lump of camphor waned, I began collecting sticks and leaves. Here and there out of the darkness round me the Morlocks' eyes shone like carbuncles.

"The camphor flickered and went out. I lit a match, and as I did so, two white forms that had been approaching Weena dashed hastily away. One was so blinded by the light that he came straight for me and I felt his bones grind under the blow of my

6 **to fizz** *here:* to produce sparks – 8 **lump** a piece of no regular shape – 24 **to encamp** to make a camp – 28 **carbuncles** bright-red jewels – 30 **to dash** to run quickly and suddenly

95

fist. He gave a whoop of dismay, staggered a little way, and fell down. I lit another piece of camphor, and went on gathering my bonfire. Presently I noticed how dry was some of the foliage above me, for since my arrival on the Time Machine, a matter

5 of a week, no rain had fallen. So, instead of casting about among the trees for fallen twigs, I began leaping up and dragging down branches. Very soon I had a choking smoky fire of green wood and dry sticks, and could economise my camphor. Then I turned to where Weena lay beside my iron mace. I tried what I could

10 to revive her, but she lay like one dead. I could not even satisfy myself whether or not she breathed.

"Now, the smoke of the fire beat over towards me, and it must have made me heavy of a sudden. Moreover, the vapour of camphor was in the air. My fire would not need replenishing for

15 an hour or so. I felt very weary after my exertion, and sat down. The wood, too, was full of a slumbrous murmur that I did not understand. I seemed just to nod and open my eyes. But all was dark, and the Morlocks had their hands upon me. Flinging off their clinging fingers I hastily felt in my pocket for the match-

20 box, and — it had gone! Then they gripped and closed with me again. In a moment I knew what had happened. I had slept, and my fire had gone out, and the bitterness of death came over my soul. The forest seemed full of the smell of burning wood. I was caught by the neck, by the hair, by the arms, and pulled down.

25 It was indescribably horrible in the darkness to feel all these soft creatures heaped upon me. I felt as if I was in a monstrous spider's web. I was overpowered, and went down. I felt little teeth nipping at my neck. I rolled over, and as I did so my hand came against my iron lever. It gave me strength. I struggled up,

---

1 **whoop** loud cry – 3 **bonfire** large fire in the open air – 3 **foliage** leaves – 5 **to cast about for** to search for s.th. in all directions – 7 **choking** making one struggle to breathe – 13 **vapour of camphor** camphor in the form of gas – 14 **to replenish** *here:* to put more wood on – 15 **exertion** effort – 20 **to close with s.o.** *lit.* to begin to fight – 27 **spider** eight-legged creature which makes a net (web) to catch insects – 28 **to nip** to try to bite

shaking the human rats from me, and, holding the bar short, I thrust where I judged their faces might be. I could feel the succulent giving of flesh and bone under my blows, and for a moment I was free.

5   "The strange exultation that so often seems to accompany hard fighting came upon me. I knew that both I and Weena were lost, but I determined to make the Morlocks pay for their meat. I stood with my back to a tree, swinging the iron bar before me. The whole wood was full of the stir and cries of them. A minute
10 passed. Their voices seemed to rise to a higher pitch of excitement, and their movements grew faster. Yet none came within reach. I stood glaring at the blackness. Then suddenly came hope. What if the Morlocks were afraid? And close on the heels of that came a strange thing. The darkness seemed to grow
15 luminous. Very dimly I began to see the Morlocks about me — three battered at my feet — and then I recognised, with incredulous surprise, that the others were running, in an incessant stream, as it seemed, from behind me, and away through the wood in front. And their backs seemed no longer
20 white, but reddish. As I stood agape, I saw a little red spark go drifting across a gap of starlight between the branches, and vanish. And at that I understood the smell of burning wood, the slumbrous murmur that was growing now into a gusty roar, the red glow, and the Morlocks' flight.
25   "Stepping out from behind my tree and looking back, I saw, through the black pillars of the nearer trees, the flames of the burning forest. It was my first fire coming after me. With that I looked for Weena, but she was gone. The hissing and crackling behind me, the explosive thud as each fresh tree burst into flame,
30 left little time for reflection. My iron bar still gripped, I followed

---

2 **succulent** juicy, fleshy – 3 **to give** *here:* to move, to bend, to break under pressure –
5 **exultation** delight, joy – 10 **pitch** level – 16 **battered** beaten, killed – 18 **incessant**
endless – 20 **agape** [əˈɡeɪp] full of amazement – 23 **gusty** stormy

in the Morlocks' path. It was a close race. Once the flames crept forward so swiftly on my right as I ran that I was outflanked and had to strike off to the left. But at last I emerged upon a small open space, and as I did so, a Morlock came blundering towards
5 me, and past me, and went on straight into the fire!

"And now I was to see the most weird and horrible thing, I think, of all that I beheld in that future age. This whole space was as bright as day with the reflection of the fire. In the centre was a hillock or tumulus, surmounted by a scorched hawthorn.
10 Beyond this was another arm of the burning forest, with yellow tongues already writhing from it, completely encircling the space with a fence of fire. Upon the hillside were some thirty or forty Morlocks, dazzled by the light and heat, and blundering hither and thither against each other in their bewilderment. At first I
15 did not realise their blindness, and struck furiously at them with my bar, in a frenzy of fear, as they approached me, killing one and crippling several more. But when I had watched the gestures of one of them groping under the hawthorn against the red sky, and heard their moans, I was assured of their absolute
20 helplessness and misery in the glare, and I struck no more of them.

"Yet every now and then one would come straight towards me, setting loose a quivering horror that made me quick to elude him. At one time the flames died down somewhat, and I feared
25 the foul creatures would presently be able to see me. I was even thinking of beginning the fight by killing some of them before this should happen; but the fire burst out again brightly, and I

---

1 **a close race** a narrow escape – 2 **to outflank** to go round the side and surprise s.o. –
4 **to blunder** to move unsteadily as if blind – 6 **weird** [wɪəd] strange, unnatural –
9 **hillock** little hill – 9 **tumulus** large pile of earth heaped over a grave – 9 **surmounted by s.th.** with s.th. on top – 9 **to scorch** to burn on the surface – 9 **hawthorn** a kind of tree or bush with small red berries – 11 **to writhe** to twist about as if in pain –
14 **bewilderment** confusion – 17 **to cripple** to injure seriously – 19 **moan** low sound of pain and suffering – 23 **to set loose** to stir up, to cause – 23 **to quiver** to tremble –
23 **to elude** to avoid, to escape

stayed my hand. I walked about the hill among them and avoided them, looking for some trace of Weena. But Weena was gone.

"At last I sat down on the summit of the hillock, and watched this strange incredible company of blind things groping to and
5 fro, and making uncanny noises to each other, as the glare of the fire beat on them.

The coiling uprush of smoke streamed across the sky, and through the rare tatters of that red canopy, remote as though they belonged to another universe, shone the little stars. Two or
10 three Morlocks came blundering into me, and I drove them off with blows of my fists, trembling as I did so.

"For the most part of that night I was persuaded it was a nightmare. I bit myself and screamed in a passionate desire to awake. I beat the ground with my hands, and got up and sat
15 down again, and wandered here and there, and again sat down. Then I would fall to rubbing my eyes and calling upon God to let me awake. Thrice I saw Morlocks put their heads down in a kind of agony and rush into the flames. But, at last, above the subsiding red of the fire, above the streaming masses of black
20 smoke and the whitening and blackening tree stumps, and the diminishing numbers of these dim creatures, came the white light of the day.

"I searched again for traces of Weena, but there were none. It was plain that they had left her poor little body in the forest. I
25 cannot describe how it relieved me to think that it had escaped the awful fate to which it seemed destined. As I thought of that, I was almost moved to begin a massacre of the helpless abominations about me, but I contained myself. The hillock, as I have said, was a kind of island in the forest. From its summit
30 I could now make out through a haze of smoke the Palace of

1 **to stay one's hand** to hold oneself back from doing s.th. unpleasant – 3 **summit** top – 5 **uncanny** strange, not natural – 7 **to coil** to form a ring or spiral – 8 **canopy** a cover on posts, usually over a bed or seat – 19 **to subside** to sink down slowly – 28 **abomination** very nasty, hateful thing

Green Porcelain, and from that I could get my bearings for the White Sphinx. And so, leaving the remnant of these damned souls still going hither and thither and moaning, as the day grew clearer, I tied some grass about my feet and limped on across smoking ashes and among black stems, that still pulsated internally with fire, towards the hiding-place of the Time Machine. I walked slowly, for I was almost exhausted, as well as lame, and I felt the intensest wretchedness for the horrible death of little Weena. It seemed an overwhelming calamity. Now, in this old familiar room, it is more like the sorrow of a dream than an actual loss. But that morning it left me absolutely lonely again — terribly alone. I began to think of this house of mine, of this fireside, of some of you, and with such thoughts came a longing that was pain.

"But, as I walked over the smoking ashes under the bright morning sky, I made a discovery. In my trouser pocket were still some loose matches. The box must have leaked before it was lost.

10

"About eight or nine in the morning I came to the same seat of yellow metal from which I had viewed the world upon the evening of my arrival. I thought of my hasty conclusions upon that evening and could not refrain from laughing bitterly at my confidence. Here was the same beautiful scene, the same abundant foliage, the same splendid palaces and magnificent ruins, the same silver river running between its fertile banks. The gay robes of the beautiful people moved hither and thither among the trees. Some were bathing in exactly the place where I had saved Weena, and that suddenly gave me a keen stab of

---

1 **to get one's bearings for** to find out which direction to take in order to get somewhere – 2 **remnant** those that remained – 13 **longing** strong wish – 29 **stab** feeling as if one is wounded with the point of a knife

pain. And like blots upon the landscape rose the cupolas above
the ways to the Underworld. I understood now what all the
beauty of the Over-world people covered. Very pleasant was
their day, as pleasant as the day of the cattle in the field. Like
5 the cattle, they knew of no enemies and provided against no
needs. And their end was the same.

"I grieved to think how brief the dream of the human intellect
had been. It had committed suicide. It had set itself steadfastly
towards comfort and ease, a balanced society with security and
10 permanency as its watchword, it had attained its hopes — to
come to this at last. Once, life and property must have reached
almost absolute safety. The rich had been assured of his wealth
and comfort, the toiler assured of his life and work. No doubt
in that perfect world there had been no unemployed problem,
15 no social question left unsolved. And a great quiet had
followed.

"It is a law of nature we overlook, that intellectual versatility
is the compensation for change, danger, and trouble. An animal
perfectly in harmony with its environment is a perfect
20 mechanism. Nature never appeals to intelligence until habit and
instinct are useless. There is no intelligence where there is no
change and no need of change. Only those animals partake of
intelligence that have to meet a huge variety of needs and
dangers.

25 "So, as I see it, the Upperworld man had drifted towards his
feeble prettiness, and the Underworld to mere mechanical
industry. But that perfect state had lacked one thing even for
mechanical perfection — absolute permanency. Apparently as
time went on, the feeding of the Underworld, however it was
30 effected, had become disjointed. Mother Necessity, who had

---

1 **blot** a spot that spoils s.th. beautiful – 8 **to set o.s. towards s.th.** to aim at, to try to
reach s.th. – 12 **the rich** here sg., old use: the rich man – 13 **toiler** lit. a man who does
hard work – 17 **versatility** cleverness at many different things – 18 **compensation**
balancing effect for s.th. bad or lacking – 22 **to partake of s.th.** to have a share of
s.th. – 30 **disjointed** disordered

been staved off for a few thousand years, came back again, and she began below. The Underworld being in contact with machinery, which, however perfect, still needs some little thought outside habit, had probably retained perforce rather
5   more initiative, if less of every other human character, than the upper. And when other meat failed them, they turned to what old habit had hitherto forbidden. So I say I saw it in my last view of the world of Eight Hundred and Two Thousand Seven Hundred and One. It may be as wrong an explanation as mortal wit could
10 invent. It is how the thing shaped itself to me, and as that I give it to you.

"After the fatigues, excitements, and terrors of the past days, and in spite of my grief, this seat and the tranquil view and the warm sunlight were very pleasant. I was very tired and sleepy,
15 and soon my theorising passed into dozing. Catching myself at that, I took my own hint, and spreading myself out upon the turf I had a long and refreshing sleep.

"I awoke a little before sunsetting. I now felt safe against being caught napping by the Morlocks, and, stretching myself, I came
20 on down the hill towards the White Sphinx. I had my crowbar in one hand, and the other hand played with the matches in my pocket.

"And now came a most unexpected thing. As I approached the pedestal of the sphinx I found the bronze valves were open.
25 They had slid down into grooves.

"At that I stopped short before them, hesitating to enter.

"Within was a small apartment, and on a raised place in the corner of this was the Time Machine. I had the small levers in my pocket. So here, after all my elaborate preparations for the
30 siege of the White Sphinx, was a meek surrender. I threw my iron bar away, almost sorry not to use it.

---

9 **mortal wit** human reason, the human mind – 13 **tranquil** calm, peaceful – 19 **to catch s.o. napping** to find s.o. asleep, to surprise s.o. – 25 **groove** *here:* long narrow opening in the ground – 26 **to stop short** to stop abruptly – 29 **elaborate** carefully worked out – 30 **siege** blockade of a strongly defended place – 30 **meek** gentle, without protest – 30 **surrender** giving up to an enemy

"A sudden thought came into my head as I stooped towards the portal. For once, at least, I grasped the mental operations of the Morlocks. Suppressing a strong inclination to laugh, I stepped through the bronze frame and up to the Time Machine.
5   I was surprised to find it had been carefully oiled and cleaned. I have suspected since that the Morlocks had even partially taken it to pieces while trying in their dim way to grasp its purpose.

"Now as I stood and examined it, finding a pleasure in the mere touch of the contrivance, the thing I had expected
10 happened. The bronze panels suddenly slid up and struck the frame with a clang. I was in the dark — trapped. So the Morlocks thought. At that I chuckled gleefully.

"I could already hear their murmuring laughter as they came towards me. Very calmly I tried to strike the match. I had only
15 to fix on the levers and depart then like a ghost. But I had overlooked one little thing. The matches were of that abominable kind that light only on the box.

"You may imagine how all my calm vanished. The little brutes were close upon me. One touched me. I made a sweeping blow
20 in the dark at them with the levers, and began to scramble into the saddle of the machine. Then came one hand upon me and then another. Then I had simply to fight against their persistent fingers for my levers, and at the same time feel for the studs over which these fitted. One, indeed, they almost got away from
25 me. As it slipped from my hand, I had to butt in the dark with my head — I could hear the Morlock's skull ring — to recover it. It was a nearer thing than the fight in the forest, I think, this last scramble.

"But at last the lever was fixed and pulled over. The clinging
30 hands slipped from me. The darkness presently fell from my eyes. I found myself in the same grey light and tumult I have already described.

---

11 **clang** loud ringing sound – 12 **gleefully** with joy and satisfaction – 20 **to scramble** to climb quickly – 22 **persistent** continuing to struggle – 23 **stud** metal part shaped like a thick flat-topped nail – 25 **to butt** to strike or push (with one's head) – 27 **nearer** *here:* even more dangerous

11

"I have already told you of the sickness and confusion that comes with time travelling. And this time I was not seated properly in the saddle, but sideways and in an unstable fashion.
5 For an indefinite time I clung to the machine as it swayed and vibrated, quite unheeding how I went, and when I brought myself to look at the dials again I was amazed to find where I had arrived. One dial records days, another thousands of days, another millions of days, and another thousands of millions.
10 Now, instead of reversing the levers I had pulled them over so as to go forward with them, and when I came to look at these indicators I found that the thousands hand was sweeping round as fast as the seconds hand of a watch — into futurity.

"As I drove on, a peculiar change crept over the appearance
15 of things. The palpitating greyness grew darker; then — though I was still travelling with prodigious velocity — the blinking succession of day and night, which was usually indicative of a slower pace, returned, and grew more and more marked. This puzzled me very much at first. The alternations of night and day
20 grew slower and slower, and so did the passage of the sun across the sky, until they seemed to stretch through centuries. At last a steady twilight brooded over the earth, a twilight only broken now and then when a comet glared across the darkling sky. The band of light that had indicated the sun had long since
25 disappeared; for the sun had ceased to set — it simply rose and fell in the west, and grew ever broader and more red. All trace of the moon had vanished. The circling of the stars, growing slower and slower, had given place to creeping points of light. At last, some time before I stopped, the sun, red and very large,

6 **unheeding** *formal:* not paying attention to – 10 **to reverse** to pull in the opposite direction – 12 **hand** *here:* the pointer of a dial – 16 **prodigious** enormous – 16 **velocity** speed – 16 **to blink** *here:* to come and go (of the light) – 18 **marked** noticeable – 19 **alternation** regular change – 22 **to brood over** to lie over s.th. (like a depressed mood) – 23 **darkling** *lit.* dark – 28 **to give place to** to disappear and change to s.th. new

halted motionless upon the horizon, a vast dome glowing with a dull heat, and now and then suffering a momentary extinction. At one time it had for a little while glowed more brilliantly again, but it speedily reverted to its sullen red heat. I

5 perceived by this slowing down of its rising and setting that the work of the tidal drag was done. The earth had come to rest with one face to the sun, even as in our own time the moon faces the earth. Very cautiously, for I remembered my former headlong fall, I began to reverse my motion. Slower and slower went the

10 circling hands until the thousands one seemed motionless and the daily one was no longer a mere mist upon its scale. Still slower, until the dim outlines of a desolate beach grew visible.

"I stopped very gently and sat upon the Time Machine, looking round. The sky was no longer blue. North-eastward it was inky

15 black, and out of the blackness shone brightly and steadily the pale white stars. Overhead it was a deep Indian red and starless, and south-eastward it grew brighter to a glowing scarlet where, cut by the horizon, lay the huge hull of the sun, red and motionless. The rocks about me were of a harsh reddish colour,

20 and all the trace of life that I could see at first was the intensely green vegetation that covered every projecting point on their south-eastern face. It was the same rich green that one sees on forest moss or on the lichen in caves: plants which like these grow in a perpetual twilight.

25 "The machine was standing on a sloping beach. The sea stretched away to the south-west, to rise into a sharp bright horizon against the wan sky. There were no breakers and no waves, for not a breath of wind was stirring. Only a slight oily

1 **dome** *here:* a shape like a rounded roof – 4 **to revert to** to return to – 4 **sullen** dark and unpleasant – 6 **tidal drag** the slowing down of the earth's circular movement by the rise and fall of the seas that is caused by the pull of the moon and the sun – 8 **cautiously** carefully and slowly – 12 **desolate** lonely, neglected – 17 **scarlet** bright red – 18 **hull** body, mass (like that of a ship) – 23 **lichen** ['laɪkən] dry-looking flat plant that spreads over stones and trees – 27 **wan** [wɒn] *lit.* pale and ill – 27 **breaker** large wave with a white top

swell rose and fell like a gentle breathing, and showed that the eternal sea was still moving and living. And along the margin where the water sometimes broke was a thick incrustation of salt — pink under the lurid sky. There was a sense of oppression in my head, and I noticed that I was breathing very fast. The sensation reminded me of my only experience of mountaineering, and from that I judged the air to be more rarefied than it is now.

"Far away up the desolate slope I heard a harsh scream, and saw a thing like a huge white butterfly go slanting and fluttering up into the sky and, circling, disappear over some low hillocks beyond. The sound of its voice was so dismal that I shivered and seated myself more firmly upon the machine. Looking round me again, I saw that, quite near, what I had taken to be a reddish mass of rock was moving slowly towards me. Then I saw the thing was really a monstrous crab-like creature. Can you imagine a crab as large as yonder table, with its many legs moving slowly and uncertainly, its big claws swaying, its long antennae, like carters' whips, waving and feeling, and its stalked eyes gleaming at you on either side of its metallic front? Its back was corrugated and ornamented with ungainly bosses, and a greenish incrustation blotched it here and there. I could see the many palps of its complicated mouth flickering and feeling as it moved.

---

1 **swell** slow rise and fall of the sea's surface – 2 **margin** edge; *here:* shore – 3 **incrustation** a hard covering – 4 **lurid** highly coloured, suggestive of flame and smoke – 5 **oppression** sadness and anxiety – 7 **mountaineering** climbing mountains – 8 **rarefied** thinner – 10 **to slant** *here:* to move upwards – 10 **to flutter** to fly by moving the wings hurriedly or irregularly – 17 **yonder** *lit.* over there – 18 **claw** part of the crab that is used for attacking, catching and holding s.th. – 18 **antenna** *pl.* **antennae** [iː] a pair of long thin organs on the head, used for feeling – 19 **carter** a man whose job is driving a vehicle drawn by a horse – 19 **stalked** [stɔːkt] standing out on a kind of stick – 20 **corrugated** with folds, shaped like waves – 21 **ungainly** ugly – 21 **boss** round button (like that in the middle of a shield) – 22 **to blotch s.th.** to discolour s.th. with a large mark

"As I stared at this sinister apparition crawling towards me, I felt a tickling on my cheek as though a fly had lighted there. I tried to brush it away with my hand, but in a moment it returned, and almost immediately came another by my ear. I struck at
5 this, and caught something threadlike. It was drawn swiftly out of my hand. With a frightful qualm, I turned, and saw that I had grasped the antenna of another monster crab that stood just behind me. Its evil eyes were wriggling on their stalks, its mouth was all alive with appetite, and its vast ungainly claws, smeared
10 with an algal slime, were descending upon me. In a moment my hand was on the lever, and I had placed a month between myself and these monsters. But I was still on the same beach, and I saw them distinctly now as soon as I stopped. Dozens of them seemed to be crawling here and there, in the sombre light, among
15 the foliated sheets of intense green.
    "I cannot convey the sense of abominable desolation that hung over the world. The red eastern sky, the northward blackness, the salt Dead See, the stony beach crawling with these foul, slow-stirring monsters, the uniform poisonous-looking
20 green of the lichenous plants, the thin air that hurts one's lungs; all contributed to an appalling effect. I moved on a hundred years, and there was the same red sun — a little larger, a little duller — the same dying sea, the same chill air, and the same crowd of earthy crustacea creeping in and out among the green
25 weed and the red rocks. And in the westward sky I saw a curved pale line like a vast new moon.
    "So I travelled, stopping ever and again, in great strides of a thousand years or more, drawn on by the mystery of the earth's fate, watching with a strange fascination the sun grow larger
30 and duller in the westward sky, and the life of the old earth ebb

---

1 **sinister** threatening – 1 **apparition** ghost-like thing – 2 **tickling** light touch – 2 **to light** *old use:* to come down and settle – 6 **qualm** unpleasant feeling of doubt – 10 **algal** consisting of algae, i.e. a small and very simple water plant – 10 **slime** nasty, bad-smelling mud – 15 **foliated** covered with leaves – 24 **crustacea** [krʌ'steɪʃə] animals with a hard outer shell, e.g. crabs

away. At last, more than thirty million years hence, the huge red-hot dome of the sun had come to obscure nearly a tenth part of the darkling heavens. Then I stopped once more, for the crawling multitude of crabs had disappeared, and the red beach,
5 save for its livid green liverworts and lichens, seemed lifeless. And now it was flecked with white. A bitter cold assailed me. Rare white flakes ever and again came eddying down. To the north-eastward, the glare of snow lay under the starlight of the sable sky, and I could see an undulating crest of hillocks pinkish
10 white. There were fringes of ice along the sea margin, with drifting masses further out; but the main expanse of that salt ocean, all bloody under the eternal sunset, was still unfrozen.

"I looked about me to see if any traces of animal life remained. A certain indefinable apprehension still kept me in the saddle
15 of the machine. But I saw nothing moving, in earth or sky or sea. The green slime on the rocks alone testified that life was not extinct. A shallow sand-bank had appeared in the sea and the water had receded from the beach. I fancied I saw some black object flopping about upon this bank, but it became
20 motionless as I looked at it, and I judged that my eye had been deceived, and that the black object was merely a rock. The stars in the sky were intensely bright and seemed to me to twinkle very little.

"Suddenly I noticed that the circular westward outline of the
25 sun had changed; that a concavity, a bay, had appeared in the curve. I saw this grow larger. For a minute perhaps I stared aghast at this blackness that was creeping over the day, and then I realised that an eclipse was beginning. Either the moon or the

---

2 **red-hot** so hot that it shines red like heated metal – 2 **to obscure** to make impossible to see, to hide – 5 **livid** very pale, bluish – 5 **liverwort** a small mossy plant growing in water or on tree-trunks – 6 **to assail** to attack violently – 9 **sable** *poet.* black or very dark and gloomy – 9 **to undulate** to rise and fall like waves – 10 **fringe** narrow strip along an edge – 11 **expanse** wide and open space – 19 **to flop about** to move around heavily and clumsily – 25 **concavity** s.th. that is curved inward – 26 **aghast** filled with fear or surprise – 28 **eclipse** total or partial cutting off of sun's light (when the moon comes between it and the earth)

planet Mercury was passing across the sun's disk. Naturally, at first I took it to be the moon, but there is much to incline me to believe that what I really saw was the transit of an inner planet passing very near to the earth.

5   "The darkness grew apace; a cold wind began to blow in freshening gusts from the east, and the showering white flakes in the air increased in number. From the edge of the sea came a ripple and whisper. Beyond these lifeless sounds the world was silent. Silent? It would be hard to convey the stillness of it.
10 All the sounds of man, the bleating of sheep, the cries of birds, the hum of insects, the stir that makes the background of our lives — all that was over. As the darkness thickened, the eddying flakes grew more abundant, dancing before my eyes; and the cold of the air more intense. At last, one by one, swiftly, one after
15 the other, the white peaks of the distant hills vanished into blackness. The breeze rose to a moaning wind. I saw the black central shadow of the eclipse sweeping towards me. In another moment the pale stars alone were visible. All else was rayless obscurity. The sky was absolutely black.
20   "A horror of this great darkness came on me. The cold, that smote to my marrow, and the pain I felt in breathing, overcame me. I shivered, and a deadly nausea seized me. Then like a red-hot bow in the sky appeared the edge of the sun. I got off the machine to recover myself. I felt giddy and incapable of facing
25 the return journey. As I stood sick and confused I saw again the moving thing upon the shoal — there was no mistake now that it was a moving thing — against the red water of the sea. It was a round thing, the size of a football perhaps, or, it may be, bigger, and tentacles trailed down from it; it seemed black against the

---

3 **transit** passing – 5 **apace** *lit*. quickly – 8 **ripple** sound of gently moving water – 21 **to smite, smote, smitten** *lit*. to strike, hit, have a powerful effect on – 21 **marrow** soft substance in the hollow parts of bones – 24 **giddy** feeling that everything is turning round – 26 **shoal** underwater bank of sand, shallow place in the sea – 29 **tentacle** long snake-like part of an animal used for feeling and seizing – 29 **to trail** to hang down, drag behind

weltering blood-red water, and it was hopping fitfully about. Then I felt I was fainting. But a terrible dread of lying helpless in that remote and awful twilight sustained me while I clambered upon the saddle.

12

"So I came back. For a long time I must have been insensible upon the machine. The blinking succession of the days and nights was resumed, the sun got golden again, the sky blue. I breathed with greater freedom. The fluctuating contours of the land ebbed and flowed. The hands spun backward upon the dials. At last I saw again the dim shadows of houses, the evidences of decadent humanity. These, too, changed and passed, and others came. Presently, when the million dial was at zero, I slackened speed. I began to recognise our own petty and familiar architecture, the thousands hand ran back to the starting-point, the night and day flapped slower and slower. Then the old walls of the laboratory came round me. Very gently, now, I slowed the mechanism down.

"I saw one little thing that seemed odd to me. I think I have told you that when I set out, before my velocity became very high, Mrs. Watchett had walked across the room, travelling, as it seemed to me, like a rocket. As I returned, I passed again across that minute when she traversed the laboratory. But now her every motion appeared to be the exact inversion of her previous ones. The door at the lower end opened, and she glided quietly up the laboratory, back foremost, and disappeared behind the door by which she had previously entered. Just before that I seemed to see Hillyer for a moment; but he passed like a flash.

---

1 **to welter** to roll – 1 **fitful** occurring in short periods, irregular – 9 **to fluctuate** to change – 9 **contours** shape, outline – 14 **to slacken** to reduce – 14 **petty** unimportant, on a small scale – 23 **to traverse** to pass through – 26 **foremost** first – 28 **Hillyer** name of a servant

"Then I stopped the machine, and saw about me again the old familiar laboratory, my tools, my appliances just as I had left them. I got off the thing very shakily, and sat down upon my bench. For several minutes I trembled violently. Then I became calmer. Around me was my old workshop again, exactly as it had been. I might have slept there, and the whole thing have been a dream.

"And yet, not exactly! The thing had started from the south-east corner of the laboratory. It had come to rest again in the north-west, against the wall where you saw it. That gives you the exact distance from my little lawn to the pedestal of the White Sphinx, into which the Morlocks had carried my machine.

"For a time my brain went stagnant. Presently I got up and came through the passage here, limping, because my heel was still painful, and feeling sorely begrimed. I saw the *Pall Mall Gazette* on the table by the door. I found the date was indeed today, and looking at the timepiece, saw the hour was almost eight o'clock. I heard your voices and the clatter of plates. I hesitated — I felt so sick and weak. Then I sniffed good wholesome meat, and opened the door on you. You know the rest. I washed, and dined, and now I am telling you the story."

"I know," he said, after a pause, "that all this will be absolutely incredible to you. To me the one incredible thing is that I am here tonight in this old familiar room, looking into your friendly faces and telling you these strange adventures."

He looked at the Medical Man. "No. I cannot expect you to believe it. Take it as a lie — or a prophecy. Say I dreamed it in the workshop. Consider I have been speculating upon the destinies of our race until I have hatched this fiction. Treat my

---

3 **shakily** unsteadily, weakly – 14 **stagnant** inactive – 16 **sorely** terribly, very –
16 **begrimed** covered with dirt – 16 **Pall Mall Gazette** a newspaper – 18 **timepiece**
clock – 20 **to sniff** to smell – 28 **prophecy** statement about the future – 30 **to hatch**
here: to give birth to s.th.

assertion of its truth as a mere stroke of art to enhance its interest. And taking it as a story, what do you think of it?"

He took up his pipe, and began, in his old accustomed manner, to tap with it nervously upon the bars of the grate. There was a momentary stillness. Then chairs began to creak and shoes to scrape upon the carpet. I took my eyes off the Time Traveller's face, and looked round at his audience. They were in the dark, and little spots of colour swam before them. The Medical Man seemed absorbed in the contemplation of our host. The Editor was looking hard at the end of his cigar — the sixth. The Journalist fumbled for his watch. The others, as far as I remember, were motionless.

The Editor stood up with a sigh. "What a pity it is you're not a writer of stories!" he said, putting his hand on the Time Traveller's shoulder.

"You don't believe it?"

"Well—"

"I thought not."

The Time Traveller turned to us. "Where are the matches?" he said. He lit one and spoke over his pipe, puffing. "To tell you the truth … I hardly believe it myself. … And yet…"

His eye fell with a mute inquiry upon the withered white flowers upon the little table. Then he turned over the hand holding his pipe, and I saw he was looking at some half-healed scars on his knuckles.

The Medical Man rose, came to the lamp, and examined the flowers. "The gynaeceum's odd," he said. The Psychologist leant forward to see, holding out his hand for a specimen.

"I'm hanged if it isn't a quarter to one," said the Journalist. "How shall we get home?"

"Plenty of cabs at the station," said the Psychologist.

---

1 **assertion** claim – 1 **to enhance** to increase – 4 **grate** metal frame for fireplace – 5 **to creak** to make a noise like a badly-oiled door – 9 **absorbed in** giving all one's attention to – 9 **contemplation** looking at and thinking deeply about – 22 **mute** silent, wordless – 27 **gynaeceum** [ˌgaɪnəˈsiːəm] the female organs of a flower – 31 **cab** *here:* horse-drawn carriage for hire

"It's a curious thing," said the Medical Man; "but I certainly don't know the natural order of these flowers. May I have them?"

The Time Traveller hesitated. Then suddenly: "Certainly not."

"Where did you really get them?" said the Medical Man.

The Time Traveller put his hand to his head. He spoke like one who was trying to keep hold of an idea that eluded him. "They were put into my pocket by Weena, when I travelled into Time." He stared round the room. "I'm damned if it isn't all going. This room and you and the atmosphere of every day is too much for my memory. Did I ever make a Time Machine, or a model of a Time Machine? Or is it all only a dream? They say life is a dream, a precious poor dream at times — but I can't stand another that won't fit. It's madness. And where did the dream come from?… I must look at that machine. If there *is* one!"

He caught up the lamp swiftly, and carried it, flaring red, through the door into the corridor. We followed him. There in the flickering light of the lamp was the machine sure enough, squat, ugly, and askew; a thing of brass, ebony, ivory, and translucent glimmering quartz. Solid to the touch — for I put out my hand and felt the rail of it — and with brown spots and smears upon the ivory, and bits of grass and moss upon the lower parts, and one rail bent awry.

The Time Traveller put the lamp down on the bench, and ran his hand along the damaged rail. "It's all right now," he said. "The story I told you was true. I'm sorry to have brought you out here in the cold." He took up the lamp, and, in an absolute silence, we returned to the smoking-room.

He came into the hall with us and helped the Editor on with his coat. The Medical Man looked into his face and, with a certain hesitation, told him he was suffering from overwork, at which

---

2 **the natural order** the group of plants to which they (the flowers) belong –
14 **precious poor** very bad – 20 **squat** [ɒ] short and thick – 20 **ebony** hard, black wood – 24 **awry** [əˈraɪ] twisted, out of the straight

he laughed hugely. I remember him standing in the open doorway, bawling good night.

I shared a cab with the Editor. He thought the tale a "gaudy lie." For my own part I was unable to come to a conclusion.
5 The story was so fantastic and incredible, the telling so credible and sober. I lay awake most of the night thinking about it. I determined to go next day and see the Time Traveller again. I was told he was in the laboratory, and being on easy terms in the house, I went up to him. The laboratory, however, was empty.
10 I stared for a minute at the Time Machine and put out my hand and touched the lever. At that the squat substantial-looking mass swayed like a bough shaken by the wind. Its instability startled me extremely, and I had a queer reminiscence of the childish days when I used to be forbidden to meddle. I came back through
15 the corridor. The Time Traveller met me in the smoking-room. He was coming from the house. He had a small camera under one arm and a knapsack under the other. He laughed when he saw me, and gave me an elbow to shake. "I'm frightfully busy," said he, "with that thing in there."
20 "But is it not some hoax?" I said. "Do you really travel through time?"

"Really and truly I do." And he looked frankly into my eyes. He hesitated. His eye wandered about the room. "I only want half an hour," he said. "I know why you came, and it's awfully
25 good of you. There's some magazines here. If you'll stop to lunch I'll prove you this time travelling up to the hilt, specimens and all. If you'll forgive my leaving you now?"

I consented, hardly comprehending then the full import of his words, and he nodded and went on down the corridor. I
30 heard the door of the laboratory slam, seated myself in a chair, and took up a daily paper. What was he going to do before

---

2 **to bawl** to shout in a loud voice – 3 **gaudy** tastelessly exaggerated, showy – 6 **sober** serious, thoughtful – 8 **on easy terms** *here:* on good or familiar terms – 14 **to meddle** to touch s.th. which is not one's own or one's concern – 16 **from the house** i.e. not the laboratory – 17 **knapsack** rucksack – 20 **hoax** trick played for a joke – 26 **up to the hilt** completely

lunchtime? Then suddenly I was reminded by an advertisement that I had promised to meet Richardson, the publisher, at two. I looked at my watch, and saw that I could barely save that engagement. I got up and went down the passage to tell the Time Traveller.

As I took hold of the handle of the door I heard an exclamation, oddly truncated at the end, and a click and a thud. A gust of air whirled round me as I opened the door, and from within came the sound of broken glass falling on the floor. The Time Traveller was not there. I seemed to see a ghostly, indistinct figure sitting in a whirling mass of black and brass for a moment — a figure so transparent that the bench behind with its sheets of drawings was absolutely distinct; but this phantasm vanished as I rubbed my eyes. The Time Machine had gone. Save for a subsiding stir of dust, the further end of the laboratory was empty. A pane of the skylight had, apparently, just been blown in.

I felt an unreasonable amazement. I knew that something strange had happened, and for the moment could not distinguish what the strange thing might be. As I stood staring, the door into the garden opened, and the man-servant appeared.

We looked at each other. Then ideas began to come. "Has Mr. — gone out that way?" said I.

"No, sir. No one has come out this way. I was expecting to find him here."

At that I understood. At the risk of disappointing Richardson I stayed on, waiting for the Time Traveller; waiting for the second, perhaps still stranger story, and the specimens and photographs he would bring with him. But I am beginning now to fear that I must wait a lifetime. The Time Traveller vanished three years ago. And, as everybody knows now, he has never returned.

---

3 **barely** hardly – 3 **to save an engagement** to manage to be punctual at a meeting –
7 **truncated** shortened, incomplete – 13 **phantasm** phantom – 14 **to subside** to settle,
to become quiet – 15 **pane** sheet of glass – 16 **skylight** window in a sloping roof

EPILOGUE

One cannot choose but wonder. Will he ever return? It may be that he swept back into the past, and fell among the blood-drinking, hairy savages of the Age of Unpolished Stone; into the abysses of the Cretaceous Sea; or among the grotesque saurians, the huge reptilian brutes of the Jurassic times. He may even now — if I may use the phrase — be wandering on some plesiosaurus-haunted Oolitic coral reef, or beside the lonely saline lakes of the Triassic Age. Or did he go forward, into one of the nearer ages, in which men are still men, but with the riddles of our own time answered and its wearisome problems solved? Into the manhood of the race: for I, for my own part, cannot think that these latter days of weak experiment, fragmentary theory, and mutual discord are indeed man's culminating time! I say, for my own part. He, I know — for the question had been discussed among us long before the Time Machine was made — thought but cheerlessly of the Advancement of Mankind, and saw in the growing pile of civilisation only a foolish heaping that must inevitably fall back upon and destroy its makers in the end. If that is so, it remains for us to live as though it were not so. But to me the future is

1 **epilogue** last part of a work of literature, here provided by the narrator – 4 **Age of Unpolished Stone** early paleolithic period, Old Stone Age (more than 10,000 years ago) – 5 **abyss** hole so deep that it appears bottomless – 5 **Cretaceous Sea** period when the chalk-rocks were formed and the giant reptiles became extinct (70,000,000–135,000,000 years ago) – 6 **Jurassic times** period characterized by the presence of dinosaurs (135,000,000–180,000,000 years ago) – 8 **plesiosaurus** [ˌpliːsiəˈsɔːrəs] extinct reptile that lived in the sea – 8 **haunted** [ɔː] visited regularly (by the plesiosaurus) – 8 **Oolithic** [ˌəʊəˈlɪθɪk] Jurassic – 9 **saline** containing salt – 9 **Triassic Age** period characterized by volcanic activity (180,000,000–220,000,000 years ago) – 11 **wearisome** tiring and boring – 12 **manhood** time when a man's body and mind are fully developed – 14 **mutual discord** disagreement and struggles among men – 15 **culminating time** time of highest development – 17 **cheerlessly** *here:* sceptically, pessimistically – 18 **Advancement of Mankind** progress of the human race – 18 **pile** heap, accumulation

still black and blank — is a vast ignorance, lit at a few casual places by the memory of his story. And I have by me, for my comfort, two strange white flowers — shrivelled now, and brown and flat and brittle — to witness that even when mind and strength had gone, gratitude and a mutual tenderness still lived on in the heart of man.

---

1 **ignorance** *here:* unknown field – 4 **brittle** dry, therefore hard but easily broken

Material for Further Study

H. G. Wells and the Critics

1. H.G. Wells's Scientific Romances (1895–1900)

The Time Machine, Wells's first scientific romance, was a
brilliant literary invention which could scarcely avoid attracting
5   comment. The first notices appeared while it was still being
serialized in five parts in the *New Review,* and its author was
acclaimed in the *Review of Reviews* as a "man of genius" after
the third instalment. Its appearance in book form in July was
largely ignored, yet such reviews as it did get were generous and
10   detailed. It was Wells's ideas and not the aesthetic qualities of
his story which were felt to invite analysis. Israel Zangwill tackled
the notion of time-travelling itself, while R. H. Hutton, the veteran
Spectator critic and Christian apologist, challenged some of the
arguments about social evolution on which Wells's vision of the
15   world of Eloi and Morlocks is based. The reviewer in *Nature* saw
it as a useful lesson in applied scientific reasoning:

Apart from its merits as a clever piece of imagination, the story is well worth
the attention of the scientific reader, for the reason that it is based so far as
possible on scientific data, and while not taking it too seriously, it helps one
20   to get a connected idea of the possible results of the ever-continuing processes
of evolution.

The notion of "science fiction" did not yet exist, and Wells
would not be seen as pioneering a new genre until much later.
Yet from the beginning his stories were recognized as appealing

---

3 **romance** a story of love, adventure, strange happenings etc., often set in a distant
time or place, in which the events are like those in a dream rather than in real life –
5 **notice** *here:* a comment in a newspaper on a new book or play, review – 11 **Israel
Zangwill** (1864–1926) Jewish English novelist and dramatist – 13 **apologist** person who
defends a belief by argument – 23 **to pioneer** to start, to develop s.th. new – 23 **genre**
['ʒɑːnrə] a category of literature (here: science fiction)

to the "scientific reader". They continued to be reviewed in *Nature,* and their scientific basis was sometimes the subject of expert discussion. At the same time readers were warned against taking them too seriously. While *The Time Machine* attracted
5   attention by means of its startling ideas, the reviewers of Wells's romances can be divided into those who read them as moral allegory and the majority who judged them as light entertainment. Following the success of Stevenson, Kipling and Rider Haggard, the entertaining romance or short story was one of the main
10 critical demands of the 1890s. Aesthetes and popular journalists were united in their dislike of the moral seriousness and sordidly factual approach of the realistic novelists. This was the period of the fireside tale of mystery or adventure, of ghost stories (even Henry James wrote *The Turn of the Screw)* and of children's
15 classics. The earliest notice of *The Time Machine* spoke of Wells as a successor of Poe, and adjectives such as "gruesome", "weird" and "horrible" abounded in the reviews. The first substantial critical article on Wells described him as a "professor of the gruesome" and a "past master in the art of producing
20 creepy sensations". His brilliant combination of creepiness and scientific subject-matter gave Wells a growing prominence among the young romancers of the time.

From the introduction to *H. G. Wells: The Critical Heritage*, ed. by Patrick Parrinder, London: Routledge & Kegan Paul, 1972, pp. 8–9.

6 **moral allegory** a text in which the characters and actions represent moral concepts – 8 **Stevenson,** Robert Louis (1850–94), author of travel books, short stories and novels, of which *Treasure Island* (1883) and *The Strange Case of Dr. Jekyll and Mr. Hyde* (1886) made him famous – 8 **Kipling,** Rudyard (1865–1936), author whose fame rests mainly on his stories about India, the sea, the jungle and its beasts; cf. *The Jungle Book* (1894) – 8 **Rider Haggard** (1856–1925), author of many popular romances, e.g. *King Solomon's Mines* (1886) – 11 **sordid** unpleasant; dirty and poor – 13 **fireside tale** story which is read to the whole family seated around the fireside – 14 **Henry James** (1843–1916), American-born, cosmopolitan writer who after 1876 mainly lived in London; a pioneer of modern psychological realism. *The Turn of the Screw* (1898) is a mysterious tale of apparitions – 16 **Poe,** Edgar Allan (1809–1849), American author. His stories fall into two categories, those of horror and those of detection. – 20 **creepy** frightful – 20 **sensation** feeling

Science Fiction and Science

2. Preface to the Scientific Romances

The following extracts are from the introduction to The
Scientific Romances of H.G. Wells *(1933). It presents Wells's fullest*
5 *critical statement about the nature and method of his science*
fiction.

These tales have been compared with the work of Jules Verne
and there was a disposition on the part of literary journalists at
one time to call me the English Jules Verne. As a matter of fact
10 there is no literary resemblance whatever between the
anticipatory inventions of the great Frenchman and these
fantasies. His work dealt almost always with actual possibilities
of invention and discovery, and he made some remarkable
forecasts. The interest he invoked was a practical one; he wrote
15 and believed and told that this or that thing could be done,
which was not at that time done. He helped his reader to imagine
it done and to realize what fun, excitement or mischief would
ensue. Many of his inventions have "come true". But these stories
of mine collected here do not pretend to deal with possible
20 things; they are exercises of the imagination in a quite different
field. They belong to a class of writing which includes the *Golden
Ass of Apuleius*, the *True Histories of Lucian*, *Peter Schlemil* and
the story of *Frankenstein*. [...] They are all fantasies; they do not

---

7 **Jules Verne** (1828–1905), French novelist, who achieved great and lasting popularity
by the combination of adventure with popular science in such books as *Journey to the
Centre of the Earth* (1864), *Twenty Thousand Leagues under the Sea* (1869), or *Around the
World in Eighty Days* (1873) – 8 **disposition** tendency – 11 **anticipatory** [æn'tɪsɪpətrɪ]
describing future events or possibilities – 14 **to invoke interest** to make people
become interested – 21 **The Golden Ass** is a satiric fantasy about the metamorphosis
of a human being into an animal – 22 **Apuleius** like **Lucian** wrote in the second century
A.D. – 22 **Peter Schlemils wundersame Geschichte** (1814), by Adalbert von Chamisso,
tells the adventures of a man who sells his shadow to the devil – 23 **Frankenstein**
(1818), by Mary Shelley, tells of a student of natural history who, from dead bodies,
constructs something like a human being and gives it life

aim to project a serious possibility; they aim indeed only at the same amount of conviction as one gets in a good gripping dream. They have to hold the reader to the end by art and illusion and not by proof and argument, and the moment he closes the cover and reflects he wakes up to their impossibility.

In all this type of story the living interest lies in their non-fantastic elements and not in the invention itself. They are appeals for human sympathy quite as much as any "sympathetic" novel, and the fantastic element, the strange property or the strange world, is used only to throw up and intensify our natural reactions of wonder, fear or perplexity. [...]

For the writer of fantastic stories to help the reader to play the game properly, he must help him in every possible unobtrusive way to *domesticate* the impossible hypothesis. He must trick him into an unwary concession to some plausible assumption and get on with his story while the illusion holds. And that is where there was a certain slight novelty in my stories when first they appeared. Hitherto, except in exploration fantasies, the fantastic element was brought in by magic. [...] But by the end of last century it had become difficult to squeeze even a momentary belief out of magic any longer. It occurred to me that instead of the usual interview with the devil or a magician, an ingenious use of scientific patter might with advantage be substituted. That was no great discovery. I simply brought the fetish stuff up to date, and made it as near actual theory as possible.

From H.G. *Wells's Literary Criticism*, ed. by Patrick Parrinder and Robert M. Philmus, Brighton: The Harvester Press, 1980, pp. 240–242. © The Estate of H.G. Wells.

1 **to project** [-'-] to imagine, to describe – 2 **conviction** readiness to believe s.th. to be true – 8 **"sympathetic"** *here:* appealing to the reader's feelings – 9 **property** *here:* quality – 12 **For the writer ... to help the reader ...** If the writer ... wants to help the reader ... – 14 **to domesticate** *here:* to make s.th. acceptable – 15 **unwary** forgetting about dangers or (here) improbabilities – 20 **to squeeze** to force out (as if) by pressure – 23 **patter** *here:* fast incomprehensible talk – 25 **the fetish stuff** the magic or supernatural elements

3. A Current Idea at the Time

In 1903 Wells wrote of *The Time Machine*, "The idea of this book was first evolved in the Debating Society of these schools" (i.e. of the Royal College of Science), and the specific occasion when the idea first presented itself to Wells may have been a debate held on 14 January 1887, when a student named E.A. Hamilton-Gordon read a paper on the "Fourth Dimension". [...] Hamilton-Gordon's paper is a rather obscurely written but basically straightforward account of the possibilities of multidimensional non-Euclidean geometries: he attempts to show that in theory it is perfectly possible to invent and describe objects existing in four-dimensional space which would bear the same relation to a cube as the latter does to a plane square. Such a figure, which can be described but not represented visually, seems to be a commonplace to modern mathematicians; but in the eighties, it appears, the notion was still original and unfamiliar. Hamilton-Gordon's paper makes it clear that the term "Fourth Dimension" was applied to several different things. [...]

Discussions about the "Fourth Dimension" seem to have been in the air in the eighties, for at the end of his paper Hamilton-Gordon added the following note:

Since writing the above, a pamphlet has been put into my hands entitled, "What is the Fourth Dimension", and to my disgust I find it is an almost exact counterpart of my theory, which I had imagined to be new and original. However, since the pamphlet bears the date of publication, 1887, and the lines of this paper were drawn up in 1886, the sin of purloining cannot be laid at my door.

---

3 **to evolve** to develop gradually – 7 **paper** essay – 9 **straightforward** presented in a direct way – 10 **Euclidean** (a system of geometry) basically limited to two or three dimensions – 13 **to bear the same relation to s.th.** to be related to s.th. in the same way

The pamphlet in question was probably C.H. Hinton's *What is the Fourth Dimension?*, which had first appeared in 1884. This was the first of Hinton's series of "Scientific Romances", which appeared at intervals throughout the eighties and nineties and
5 popularized various scientific facts and possibilities. Oscar Wilde may well have been aware of Hinton's pamphlet, or some similar contemporary discussion, for in his story "The Canterville Ghost", he says of the Ghost, "There was evidently no time to be lost, so, hastily adopting the Fourth Dimension of Space as
10 a means of escape, he vanished through the wainscoting, and the house became quite quiet."
Both concepts of the Fourth Dimension — as a further dimension of space, and as duration of time — offered a good deal of scope to the writer of scientific romance, and Wells made
15 use of both of them. In *The Chronic Argonauts* and *The Time Machine* he is concerned with the Fourth Dimension as time, though in the latter work he also shows himself aware of the alternative view, and refers to the work of the distinguished American mathematician, Professor Simon Newcomb. Though
20 time travelling, as expounded [...] by the hero of *The Time Machine*, was the imaginative product of serious discussion about multidimensional geometries, it is an essentially pseudo-scientific notion, despite the immensely plausible way in which Wells treats the topic in *The Time Machine*. Van Wyck Brooks,
25 writing in 1915, said that he was unable to see what was wrong with the exposition of time travelling, but other writers had already pointed out the logical impossibility of travelling in time. Within a few months of the appearance of *The Time Machine* in 1895, Israel Zangwill had discussed at some length in a review

5 **Oscar Wilde** (1854–1900) author of poems, fiction, and witty comedies, e.g. *The Importance of Being Earnest* (1895). "The Canterville Ghost" was first published in 1887. – 9 **to adopt** *here:* to take and use – 10 **wainscoting** panelling, esp. on the lower half of the walls of a room – 15 **The Chronic Argonauts** one of Wells's earliest stories, published in 1888 – 24 **Van Wyck Brooks** (1886–1963) a noted American scholar and literary critic

the impossibility of the book's basic idea, and a more systematic refutation was given in philosophical language in 1914 by W.B. Pitkin. However, such demonstrations of the scientific impossibility of the book's underlying concept in no way detract
5 from the imaginative quality and mythical power of *The Time Machine.*

From *The Early H.G. Wells* by Bernard Bergonzi, Manchester: Manchester University Press, 1961, pp. 31–33.

4. The Fourth Dimension

10 In the modern view of the geometry of the universe, time is the fourth dimension. In this view, four numbers (coordinates) are required to identify an event in nature: three numbers to locate its position in space, and a fourth number to indicate the time of its occurrence.
15 Until the general acceptance of Einstein's special theory of relativity (1905), the designation of time as a fourth dimension was purely formal: what was length to one observer could become height to a differently oriented observer, but it was generally agreed that a time separation between two events
20 could in no sense be observed as a space separation. However, Einstein showed that events that appear simultaneous to a stationary observer are not so to a moving observer. That is, an

4 **to detract from** to make s.th. appear smaller, of less value – 11 **coordinate** [ˌkəʊˈɔːdinət] *tech:* any of an ordered set of numbers (and/or letters) that give the exact position of a point, e.g. on a map – 15 **Einstein**, Albert (1879–1955). In a famous article published in 1905 in the German scientific journal *Annalen der Physik*, Einstein used the following thought experiment: an observer standing next to a railway line sees two bolts of lightning strike the tracks at the same time, one far to the east, the other at an equal distance to the west. Another observer who passes just in front of him on a train moving at high speed from east to west perceives the same event as a flash in the west followed by one in the east. Because he is moving away from the bolt in the east, its light takes slightly longer to reach him. – 16 **designation of s.th.** as the fact of calling s.th., description of s.th. as – 17 **purely formal** not based on experience

apparently pure spatial separation can be transformed into a separation in space and time. This fact justifies the term "fourth dimension."

Encyclopedia Americana, s.v. "Fourth Dimension", contribution by Macgregor
5   Suzuki, Queens College, N.Y. Reprinted with permission of *The Encyclopedia Americana*, copyright 1983, Grolier Inc., Danbury, Connecticut.

The Social Context

By the end of the nineteenth century, industrialization had transformed Britain. The country now mainly depended on the
10 *extraction and import of raw materials and on the manufacturing of finished products, largely for export. As a consequence, the work environment, too, had changed, mine and factory replacing farm and village for a great part of the working population.*

5. Incomes and Prices

15   Did people living in the nineteenth century gain or lose from the revolution in industry?

Such simple questions are rarely easy to answer, because different people's experiences varied so much. When Victoria became queen in 1837, many hand-loom weavers' and some
20 southern farm labourers' families had been driven to the brink of starvation by the economic changes of the previous generation. In addition many others suffered at least temporarily from unemployment or the loss of their common lands. On the other hand, the growth of trade and industry had already brought
25 a marked rise in wages in most industrial counties together with handsome profits for many merchants and manufacturers, farmers and landowners.

19 **hand-loom** a frame on which thread is woven into cloth by hand – 20 **to the brink of** almost to; so that they were in danger of … – 23 **common land** land that everyone was allowed to use – 25 **marked** noticeable

By the 1840s the situation was summed up neatly by the philosopher J.S.Mill. "Hitherto," he wrote, "it is questionable if all the mechanical inventions yet made have lightened the day's toil of any human being. They have enabled a greater proportion
5 to live the same life of drudgery and imprisonment and an increased number of manufacturers and others to make fortunes."

As he was writing, however, things were changing and since then the country's standard of living has risen remarkably. [...]

10 British national income		Average annual income per person	
1850	£ 500 million	1851	£ 20
1880	£ 1,000 million	1881	£ 31
1910	£ 2,000 million	1911	£ 49

Unfortunately everybody did not share equally in the growing
15 wealth. [...] many families were still poverty-stricken at the end of the century, and even though the proportion of those who were poor fell during the second half of the nineteenth century, their total number actually increased, because the population grew so fast.

20 Four years after Queen Victoria died in 1901, L.C. Money estimated that the following groups in England and Wales each shared a third of the national income.

people	annual income	
1.4 million	over	£700
25 4.1 million		£160–700
39.0 million	under	£160

From *Britain transformed. The development of British society since the mid-eighteenth century* by V.T.J. Arkell, Harmondsworth: Penguin Education, 1973, pp. 180–181. Copyright © V.T.J. Arkell, 1973.

2 **John Stuart Mill** (1806–73). Many of his works comment on economic and political questions; cf. *Principles of Political Economy* (1848), *Liberty* (1859), or *The Subjection of Women* (1869). – 10 **annual** ['ænjʊəl] of one year – 15 **stricken** experiencing the effects of (poverty) – 20 **Money**, Sir Leo Chiozza. His book *Riches and Poverty* caused great stir when it appeared in 1905.

6. Food

In addition to banquets, when a dozen or more different meat courses might be served, the wealthy consumed huge quantities of beef, mutton, venison, pheasant, salmon and trout throughout the year. Before the late nineteenth century they ate few vegetables with them. "The Victorian upper classes came to be as fond of good food as they were of other sins of the flesh," wrote the historian Dr J. Burnett in *Plenty and Want.* "Probably no civilization since the Roman ate as well as they did. The achievements of modern science combined to place the delicacies of the world on the tables of the rich. In nothing was the contrast between wealth and poverty more obvious than in food." The comfortably-off middle classes ate substantially too, enjoying perhaps bacon and eggs for breakfast and a meat dish and suet or pastry pudding at most main meals. Novels about life in Victorian times often describe them tucking into solid meals. In Arnold Bennett's *Old Wives' Tale,* for instance, the family of a prosperous draper have cockles, mussels, toast and tea in the afternoon, followed by cold pork, apple pie and cheese for supper.

It is much more difficult to find out how the working classes fared in the growing towns, because their standard of living was so varied — as Engels discovered in Manchester in the 1840s:

The better-paid workers, especially those in whose families every member is able to earn something, have good food as long as this state of things lasts;

8 **Dr John Burnett.** *His book Plenty and Want: A Social History of Diet in England from 1815 to the Present Day appeared in 1966. – 15* **suet** ['suːɪt] a kind of hard fat from the kidneys of an animal, used together with flour, bread etc. to prepare a kind of pudding – 16 **to tuck into** informal to eat eagerly – 17 **Arnold Bennett** (1867–1931). His novels, e.g. *The Old Wives' Tale* (1908), give vivid descriptions of life in the pottery area around Stoke-upon-Trent. – 22 **to fare** to get on – 23 **Engels,** Friedrich (1820–1895). The son of a wealthy German textile manufacturer, Engels had, even before he met Karl Marx in 1844, acquired considerable insight into the plight of the working classes while working in Manchester at one of his father's factories. *The Condition of the Working Class in England* was published in German in 1845. First English translation New York 1887/London 1892.

meat daily, and bacon and cheese for supper. Where wages are less, meat is used only two or three times a week, and the proportion of bread and potatoes increases. Descending gradually, we find the animal food reduced to a small piece of bacon cut up with the potatoes; lower still, even this disappears, 5 and there remains only bread, cheese, porridge and potatoes until, on the lowest round of the ladder, potatoes form the sole food. [...]

In the 1880s the prices of most common foods fell by up to a third. Most people therefore enjoyed a more varied and purer diet.

10 The main cause was the import in huge quantities of cheap foreign wheat and meat. The early tinned meat was coarse, stringy and unappetizing, usually containing a large chunk of unpleasant-looking fat. However, it sold at half the price of most fresh meat and many families bought it happily. Soon, frozen, 15 and later chilled, beef and mutton from Australasia and the Argentine were almost as cheap and clearly of much better quality than tinned meat. Fish was also preserved in ice and so, in addition to herring, by the end of the century, a lot of cheap cod was eaten, often fried with chips. [...]

20 By 1900 the working classes spent about 2 to 4 shillings a week on food for every member of the family, while the comfortably-off middle classes enjoyed between 10 and 30 shillings each.

From *Britain transformed* by V.T.J. Arkell, pp. 184–187.

7. Domestic Service

25 The health and comfort of the better-off Victorian families depended to a large extent on their servants. Twenty or more were employed in the wealthiest houses, while women whose husbands had incomes of about £500 a year could afford three

6 **round** *here:* step of a ladder, rung – 15 **chilled** preserved by keeping cold but not frozen

full-time servants — enough to relieve them of almost all housework. The wives of most tradesmen and clerks and of some skilled workmen who earned nearly £100 a year usually had one girl for most of the heavy work, while they cooked and looked
5 after their children themselves. Few families with lower incomes kept full-time servants, although many did employ women for particular tasks like washing.

Servants had plenty to do in houses which had neither running water nor electricity, where most rooms had a coal fire and where
10 food was cooked on an open fire or kitchen range throughout the year. […]

The domestic servant in Arnold Benett's *The Old Wives' Tale* "lived seventeen hours of each day in an underground kitchen and larder, and the other seven in an attic, never going out except
15 to chapel on Sunday evenings, and once a month on Thursday afternoons. On rare occasions an aunt was permitted as a tremendous favour to see her in the subterranean den. Everybody, including herself, considered that she had a good place and was well treated."

20 Underground kitchens were usual. They were often very gloomy because they had few windows. They rarely had more furniture than a table, a few wooden chairs and the odd cupboard. The kitchen was at least warm, unlike a maid's bedroom which was usually in an attic and was often icy cold
25 in winter. "The places in which some maids are asked to sleep are a disgrace to civilization," declared the *Woman's Book* early in the twentieth century. "Underground bedrooms, besides being dark and airless, are sometimes damp and insanitary as well."

From *Britain transformed* by V.T.J. Arkell, pp. 196–197.

10 **range** iron stove in a kitchen with an oven, hot-plates, etc. – 15 **chapel** *here:* service in a church used by people who belong neither to the Anglican nor the Roman Catholic church – 17 **den** home or hiding-place of a wild animal, e.g. a cave – 22 **the odd cupboard** occasionally a cupboard – 23 **maid** female servant

8. The Urban Poor

In the 1880s, [...] a leading socialist, H.M. Hyndman, claimed that a quarter of the population was poor. Charles Booth, a wealthy Liverpool merchant and shipowner, was one of the many
5   who maintained that this was both untrue and dangerous. To prove that Hyndman was wrong, he organized a survey of every house in the east end and centre of London.

By 1889 Booth was indeed able to put Hyndman right, but not in the way he expected. Hyndman had actually
10   underestimated the amount of poverty. Booth found that just under one Londoner in three was poor. In addition a quarter of those (or nearly ten per cent altogether) lived in extreme poverty. (Of course some districts contained few poor people, but two-thirds of the population were poor in parts of Southwark.) In
15   the next twenty years investigations in York and elsewhere confirmed Booth's conclusion. Without doubt at least a quarter of the population lived in poverty.

But what did poverty mean?

For Booth "my poor may be described as living under a struggle
20   to obtain the necessaries of life and make both ends meet; while the very poor live in a state of chronic want." [...]

Why were people poor?

Many Victorians assumed that it was because they were lazy, drank or did not save. As one judge argued: "poverty could be
25   prevented if you could prevent weakness and sickness and laziness and stupidity and improvidence, not otherwise." "That drink leads to beggary as well as to crime is a commonplace,"

---

2 **Henry Mayers Hyndman** (1842–1921) founder of the Social Democratic Federation (1881) – 3 **Charles Booth** (1840–1916). The first two volumes of his sociological survey *Life and Labour of the People in London* were published in 1889 and 1891. – 5 **to maintain** to claim, to argue – 8 **to put s.o. right** to prove to s.o. that he was wrong – 14 **Southwark** ['sʌðək] central part of London south of the Thames – 15 **York** The social investigations there were carried out by B.S. Rowntree (1871–1954) and published in *Poverty: A Study of Town Life* (1901). – 20 **to make both ends meet** to make just enough money for one's needs – 26 **improvidence** failure to provide for future needs

added another writer. But the researches of Booth, Rowntree and others showed convincingly that the great majority were not poor because of their own failings. Although few families were poor for just one reason, Booth and Rowntree estimated
5 the prime causes of their poverty like this:

Booth:	66 % low wages and lack of regular work for father
	21 % too many children or one parent seriously ill
	13 % drink and thriftlessness

Rowntree:	52 % father received too low wages
10	22 % family too large (more than four children)
	21 % death or illness of the father
	5 % father out of regular work

According to Rowntree drink and gambling, ignorant or careless housekeeping all aggravated poverty, but they rarely
15 caused it.

From *Britain transformedby* V.T.J. Arkell, pp. 107–108.

9. The Dark Side of Life

We are not in the square now, but in a long, dirty street, full of lodging-houses from end to end, a perfect human warren, where
20 every door stands open night and day [...]. In this street [...] we select at hazard an open doorway and plunge into it. We pass along a greasy, grimy passage, and turn a corner to ascend the stairs. Round the corner it is dark. There is no staircase light, and we can hardly distinguish in the gloom where we are going.
25 A stumble causes us to strike a light.
    That stumble was a lucky one. The staircase we were ascending, and which men and women and little children go up and down

8 **thriftlessness** careless use of money – 19 **warren** *fig.* a place in which too many people live (almost like rabbits) – 21 **at hazard** at random, without aim or purpose – 25 **to strike a light** to light a match

day after day and night after night, is a wonderful affair. The handrail is broken away, the stairs themselves are going — a heavy boot has been clean through one of them already, and it would need very little, one would think, for the whole lot to give way and fall with a crash. A sketch, taken at the time, by the light of successive vestas, fails to give the grim horror of that awful staircase. The surroundings, the ruin, the decay, and the dirt, could not be reproduced.

We are anxious to see what kind of people get safely up and down this staircase, and as we ascend we knock accidentally up against something; it is a door and a landing. The door is opened, and as the light is thrown onto where we stand we give an involuntary exclamation of horror; the door opens right onto the corner stair. The woman who comes out would, if she stepped incautiously, fall six feet, and nothing could save her. It is a tidy room this, for the neighbourhood. A good hardworking woman has kept her home neat, even in such surroundings. The rent is four and sixpence a week, and the family living in it numbers eight souls; their total earnings are twelve shillings. A hard lot, one would fancy; but in comparison to what we have to encounter presently it certainly is not. Asked about the stairs, the woman says, "It is a little ockard-like for the young 'uns a-goin' up and down to school now the Board make 'em wear boots; but they don't often hurt themselves." Minus the boots, the children had got used to the ascent and descent, I suppose, and were as much at home on the crazy staircase as a chamois on a precipice.

From *How the Poor Live* (1883) by George R. Sims. Reprinted in Peter Keating, ed. *Into Unknown England 1866–1913. Selections from the Social Explorers*, London: Fontana/Collins, 1976, pp. 70–71.

1 **wonderful** *here:* astonishing, strange – 3 **clean through** right through – 6 **vesta** a type of match – 18 **four and sixpence** four shillings and a half – 19 **lot** what life has to offer, fate – 21 **to encounter** to meet or see unexpectedly – 22 **ockard-like** *dialect* awkward, i.e. difficult – 22 **the young 'uns** the young ones, i.e. the children – 23 **the Board** the school board, (until 1902) a local government body in charge of schools

The Struggle for Survival and Social Evolution

The Victorian belief in human progress was seriously weakened towards the turn of the century. In The Time Machine *this finds expression in various ways. Thus the Golden Age in which the*
5 *Eloi seem to live turns out to be a period of decadence and degeneration.*

The texts in this section offer various facets of the history of ideas in the nineteenth century. It is against this background of evolutionary philosophy and political economy that Wells's
10 *novel was written. The English translation of* The Communist Manifesto *appeared only seven years before the publication of* The Time Machine *and was widely read and discussed at the time.*

10. Social Darwinism

15 Few Americans living today have read any of Herbert Spencer's writings, but they had an electrifying effect on America during the last three decades of the nineteenth century — a far greater effect than in Spencer's native England. Their influence was so great, in fact, that they worked themselves into the folkways of
20 American political philosophy — into the everyday assumptions that many Americans still carry around in their heads about how social life is and should be arranged.

To Spencer and his followers, the marketplace was a field for the development and encouragement of personal character.
25 Work provided people with moral discipline, and that was critical to survival. Life, after all, was a competitive struggle in which

---

15 **Herbert Spencer** (1820–1903), the founder of evolutionary philosophy, among whose main works are his *Programme of a System of Synthetic Philosophy* (1860) and *Principles of Sociology* (1876–96) – 19 **folkways** ways of thinking that are common to a people or social group – 25 **critical to** most important for

only those with the strongest moral fiber could survive. It was through this competitive struggle that societies became stronger over time. Only the fittest were able to prosper, because only they were able to muster the necessary resources to sustain
5 themselves and their offspring.

Even before Darwin's evolutionary theories were presented to the world in 1859, Spencer had developed the idea that the pressure of subsistence upon population would have a beneficent effect upon the human race. The miserable social conditions of
10 the early industrial revolution had provided data for Malthus's grim essay on the principle of population, but Spencer saw in the thesis a cause for hope. For the very process of impoverishment would place a premium upon skill, intelligence, self-control, and the power to adapt through technological
15 innovation. The inevitable pressure of poverty would itself stimulate human advancement by selecting the best of each generation for survival. It was Spencer, not Darwin, who coined the phrase "survival of the fittest."

An inevitable correlate of this principle was that government
20 should do little or nothing to eliminate poverty. Charity was permissible; if the "fittest" wished to bestow gifts upon some of the less fit, that would not contravene evolutionary forces and might indeed enhance the moral character of the giver. But state intervention to improve the lot of the poor would have disastrous
25 results. Not only were the effects of public programs for the poor often vastly different from their intended consequences [...], but the programs themselves interfered with natural selection.

---

1 **moral fiber** (*Am. E. spelling; B.E.: fibre*) strength of character – 4 **to sustain o.s.** to keep o.s. alive and strong – 6 **Darwin,** Charles (1809–82), whose work *On the Origin of Species* was published in 1859 – 8 **the pressure of subsistence** the necessity to keep o.s. alive, to make a living – 10 **Malthus,** Thomas Robert (1766–1834). In his *Essay on the Principle of Population* (1798, 1803) he argued that population would soon increase beyond the means of subsistence and that 'natural checks' (war, famine, epidemics, vice) would limit the growth of the population. – 22 **to contravene** to act in opposition to

Spencer's follower, William Graham Sumner, a professor of political and social science at Yale [...], put the case succinctly:

If we do not like the survival of the fittest we have only one possible alternative,
5   and that is the survival of the unfittest. The former is the law of civilization.
... A plan for nourishing the unfittest and yet advancing civilization, no man will ever find.

Spencer and his followers publicly deplored poor laws, state-supported education, regulation of housing conditions, and the
10 protection of the consumer against dangers and deceptions. They also found anathema any state-enforced effort to achieve equality, even equality of opportunity, because evolution depended for its force on inequality. Those who could not adapt themselves to their environment for whatever reason should
15 not be artificially helped, so they thought, because the survival of the species depended on the survival of people who could adapt. Without natural inequalities, the law of survival of the fittest would have no meaning.

From "Ideologies of Survival" by Robert B. Reich, *The New Republic*, September
20 20 & 27, 1982, pp. 33–34.

11. The Struggle for Existence and Human Society

In the strict sense of the word "nature", it denotes the sum of the phenomenal world, of that which has been, and is, and will be; and society, like art, is therefore a part of nature. But it is
25 convenient to distinguish those parts of nature in which man

1 **William Graham Sumner** (1840–1910); the quotation is from *Earth Hunger and Other Essays* (1913) – 2 **Yale** famous private university in the United States – 8 **to deplore** to consider wrong – 8 **poor laws** ['--] laws concerning help for poor people – 11 **anathema** [ə'næθɪmə] *here:* s.th. hated – 22 **to denote** to mean – 23 **phenomenal** *here:* known through the senses

plays the part of immediate cause, as something apart; and, therefore, society, like art, is usefully to be considered as distinct from nature. It is the more desirable, and even necessary, to make the distinction, since society differs from nature in having
5 a definite moral object; whence it comes about that the course shaped by the ethical man — the member of society or citizen — necessarily runs counter to that which the non-ethical man — the primitive savage, or man as a mere member of the animal kingdom — tends to adopt. The latter fights out the
10 struggle for existence to the bitter end, like any other animal; the former devotes his best energies to the object of setting limits to the struggle.

In the cycle of phenomena presented by the life of man, the animal, no more moral end is discernible than in that presented
15 by the lives of the wolf and of the deer. However imperfect the relics of prehistoric men may be, the evidence which they afford clearly tends to the conclusion that, for thousands and thousands of years, before the origin of the oldest known civilizations, men were savages of a very low type. They strove with their enemies
20 and their competitors; they preyed upon things weaker or less cunning than themselves; they were born, multiplied without stint, and died, for thousands of generations alongside the mammoth, the urus, the lion, and the hyaena, whose lives were spent in the same way; and they were no more to be praised or
25 blamed, on moral grounds, than their less erect and more hairy compatriots.

As among these, so among primitive men, the weakest and stupidest went to the wall, while the toughest and shrewdest, those who were best fitted to cope with their circumstances, but
30 not the best in any other sense, survived. Life was a continual

---

5 **object** *here:* aim, purpose – 5 **whence** *old use:* from which fact – 5 **to come about** to happen, to result – 7 **counter** in a direction which is opposite – 14 **moral end** moral purpose – 20 **to prey upon** to hunt and catch – 21 **without stint** without limit – 23 **urus** extinct wild ox – 28 **to go to the wall** to suffer defeat, to be pushed aside

free fight, and beyond the limited and temporary relations of the family, the Hobbesian war of each against all was the normal state of existence. The human species, like others, plashed and floundered amid the general stream of evolution, keeping
5 its head above water as it best might, and thinking neither of whence nor whither.

The history of civilization — that is, of society — on the other hand, is the record of the attempts which the human race has made to escape from this position. The first men who substituted
10 the state of mutual peace for that of mutual war, whatever the motive which impelled them to take that step, created society. But, in establishing peace, they obviously put a limit upon the struggle for existence. Between the members of that society, at any rate, it was not to be pursued *à outrance*. And of all the
15 successive shapes which society has taken, that most nearly approaches perfection in which the war of individual 45 against individual is most strictly limited.

From "The Struggle for Existence in Human Society" (1888) by Thomas Henry Huxley. Reprinted in T. H. Huxley, *Evolution and Ethics and Other Essays*
20 (Collected Essays, vol. IX), New York: Greenwood, pp. 202–204.

12. *La misère* and the Renewed Struggle for Existence

It needs no argument to prove that when the price of labour sinks below a certain point, the worker infallibly falls into that condition which the French emphatically call *la misère* — a word
25 for which I do not think there is any exact English equivalent. It is a condition in which the food, warmth, and clothing which are necessary for the mere maintenance of the functions of the

---

1 **free fight** fight, usually without rules, in which anybody may join – 2 **Hobbesian** referring to the political theory of Thomas Hobbes (1588–1679), esp. to his *Leviathan* (1651) – 3 **to plash** to move in water, striking it lightly – 4 **to flounder** to move about with great difficulty, trying not to sink – 14 **à outrance** *(French)* to the extreme – 23 **infallibly** inevitably, always

body in their normal state cannot be obtained; in which men, women, and children are forced to crowd into dens wherein decency is abolished and the most ordinary conditions of healthful existence are impossible of attainment; in which the
5 pleasures within reach are reduced to bestiality and drunkenness; in which the pains accumulate at compound interest, in the shape of starvation, disease, stunted development, and moral degradation; in which the prospect of even steady and honest industry is a life of unsuccessful battling with hunger, rounded
10 by a pauper's grave.

That a certain proportion of the members of every great aggregation of mankind should constantly tend to establish and populate such a Slough of Despond as this is inevitable, so long as some people are by nature idle and vicious, while others are
15 disabled by sickness or accident, or thrown upon the world by the death of their bread-winners. So long as that proportion is restricted within tolerable limits, it can be dealt with; and, so far as it arises only from such causes, its existence may and must be patiently borne. But, when the organization of society, instead
20 of mitigating this tendency, tends to continue and intensify it; when a given social order plainly makes for evil and not for good, men naturally enough begin to think it high time to try a fresh experiment. The animal man, finding that the ethical man has landed him in such a slough, resumes his ancient sovereignty,
25 and preaches anarchy; which is, substantially, a proposal to reduce the social cosmos to chaos, and begin the brute struggle for existence once again.

---

3 **decency** conformity to moral and social standards – 6 **at compound interest** more and more rapidly, like money when interest is calculated on the original amount of capital plus all the interest already earned – 7 **stunted** prevented from growing – 9 **industry** *here:* continual hard work – 10 **a pauper's grave** poor people were formerly buried in a separate public burying-place – 12 **aggregation** number (*here* of people) come together in a group or mass – 13 **Slough of Despond** [slaʊ] "swamp of hopelessness"; the term was used metaphorically for a situation of fear, doubt, despair and misery in John Bunyan's *The Pilgrim's Progress* (1678), a Christian allegory of human life – 14 **vicious** full of evil habits – 20 **to mitigate** to lessen, to make easier to bear

Any one who is acquainted with the state of the population of all great industrial centres, whether in this or other countries, is aware that, amidst a large and increasing body of that population, *la misere* reigns supreme. I have no pretensions to
5   the character of a philanthropist, and I have a special horror of all sorts of sentimental rhetoric; I am merely trying to deal with facts, to some extent within my own knowledge, and further evidenced by abundant testimony, as a naturalist; and I take it to be a mere plain truth that, throughout industrial Europe,
10 there is not a single large manufacturing city which is free from a vast mass of people whose condition is exactly that described; and from a still greater mass who, living just on the edge of the social swamp, are liable to be precipitated into it by any lack of demand for their produce. And, with every addition to the
15 population, the multitude already sunk in the pit and the number of the host sliding towards it continually increase.

From "The Struggle for Existence in Human Society" (1888) by Thomas Henry Huxley, pp. 214–216.

13. Bourgeois and Proletarians

20 The history of all hitherto existing society is the history of class struggles.

Free man and slave, patrician and plebeian, lord and serf, guild master and journeyman, in a word, oppressor and oppressed, stood in constant opposition to one another, carried

---

4 **pretensions** claim – 5 **character** *rare:* reputation – 8 **naturalist** a person who studies living beings in their environment – 13 **to be liable** to be likely to – 16 **host** large number – 19 **bourgeois.** By "bourgeoisie" is meant the class of modern capitalists, owners of the means of social production and employers of wage labour. By proletariat, the class of modern wage labourers who, having no means of production of their own, are reduced to selling their labour in order to live. [Note by Engels to the English edition of 1888.] – 23 **guild master**, that is, a full member of a guild, a master within, not a head of a guild. [Note by Engels to the English edition of 1888.]

on an uninterrupted, now hidden, now open fight, a fight that each time ended either in a revolutionary reconstitution of society at large or in the common ruin of the contending classes.

5   In the earlier epochs of history we find almost everywhere a complicated arrangement of society into various orders, a manifold gradation of social rank. In ancient Rome we have patricians, knights, plebeians, slaves; in the Middle Ages, feudal lords, vassals, guild masters, journeymen, apprentices, serfs; in
10   almost all of these classes, again, subordinate gradations.

    The modern bourgeois society that has sprouted from the ruins of feudal society has not done away with class antagonisms. It has but established new classes, new conditions of oppression, new forms of struggle in place of the old ones.

15   Our epoch, the epoch of the bourgeoisie, possesses, however, this distinctive feature: it has simplified the class antagonisms. Society as a whole is more and more splitting up into two great hostile camps, into two great classes directly facing each other: bourgeoisie and proletariat. [Marx and Engels go on to describe
20   the development of bourgeoisie and proletariat in detail.]

    In depicting the most general phases of the development of the proletariat, we traced the more or less veiled civil war, raging within existing society, up to the point where that war breaks out into open revolution and where the violent overthrow of
25   the bourgeoisie lays the foundation for the sway of the proletariat.

    Hitherto every form of society has been based, as we have already seen, on the antagonism of opressing and oppressed classes. But in order to oppress a class certain conditions must
30   be assured to it under which it can, at least, continue its slavish existence. The serf, in the period of serfdom, raised himself to membership in the commune, just as the petty bourgeois, under

---

2 **reconstitution of society** the establishment of a new order – 11 **to sprout** to grow – 13 **but** only, just – 25 **sway** *lit.* power to rule – 32 **petty bourgeois** person of the lower middle class

the yoke of feudal absolutism, managed to develop into a bourgeois. The modern labourer, on the contrary, instead of rising with the progress of industry, sinks deeper and deeper below the conditions of existence of his own class. He becomes

5 a pauper, and pauperism develops more rapidly than population and wealth. And here it becomes evident that the bourgeoisie is unfit any longer to be the ruling class in society, and to impose its conditions of existence upon society as an overriding law. It is unfit to rule because it is incompetent to assure an existence

10 to its slave within his slavery, because it cannot help letting him sink into such a state that it has to feed him instead of being fed by him. Society can no longer live under this bourgeoisie: in other words, its existence is no longer compatible with society.

15 From *The Communist Manifesto* by Karl Marx and Friedrich Engels. Reprinted in Irving Howe, ed., *Essential Works of Socialism*, New York: Holt, Rinehart and Winston, 1970, pp. 30–31 and 42–43.

Cosmic Evolution and the End of the World

14. Retrogressive Evolution

20 It is an error to imagine that evolution signifies a constant tendency to increased perfection. That process undoubtedly involves a constant remodelling of the organism in adaptation to new conditions; but it depends on the nature of those conditions whether the direction of the modifications effected

25 shall be upward or downward. Retrogressive is as practicable as progressive metamorphosis. If what the physical philosophers

---

1 **yoke** rule or control which is hard to bear – 20 **to signify** to mean – 25 **retrogressive** (metamorphosis) which shows a return to an earlier, less advanced state – 26 **physical philosopher** theoretical physicist

tell us, that our globe has been in a state of fusion, and, like the sun, is gradually cooling down, is true, then the time must come when evolution will mean adaptation to a universal winter, and all forms of life will die out, except such low and simple
5 organisms as the Diatom of the arctic and antarctic ice and the Protococcus of the red snow. If our globe is proceeding from a condition in which it was too hot to support any but the lowest living thing to a condition in which it will be too cold to permit of the existence of any others, the course of life upon its surface
10 must describe a trajectory like that of a ball fired from a mortar; and the sinking half of that course is as much a part of the general process of evolution as the rising.

From "The Struggle for Existence in Human Society" (1888) by Thomas Henry Huxley, p. 199.

15 ## 15. The End of the World

No better introduction to late nineteenth- and early twentieth-century preoccupation with the end of the world exists than the history of the Second Law of Thermodynamics given by Henry Adams in *The Degradation of the Democratic Dogma:*

20 Towards the middle of the nineteenth century, — that is, about 1850, — a new school of physicists appeared in Europe, dating from an Essay on the Motive Power of Heat, published by Sadi Carnot in 1824, and made famous by the names of William Thomson, Lord Kelvin, in England, and of Clausius

---

1 **fusion** melting (because of great heat) – 5 **Diatom** very small water plant, a kind of alga – 6 **Protococcus** another kind of microscopically small alga – 6 **red snow** snow reddened by the presence of Protococcus, frequent in Arctic regions – 10 **mortar** short heavy cannon – 18 **Henry Adams** (1838–1918), American historian and novelist, who in *The Degradation of the Democratic Dogma* (1919) sets forth a dynamic theory of history comparable to Huxley's view of evolution – 22 **motive** causing movement – 22 **Sadi Carnot** (1796–1832), French engineer and physicist – 23 **William Thomson, Lord Kelvin** (1824–1907), British physicist – 23 **Clausius,** Rudolf (1822–1888), German physicist

and Helmholtz in Germany, who announced a second law of dynamics. The first law said that Energy was never lost; the second said that it was never saved; that, while the sum of energy in the universe might remain constant, — granting that the universe was a closed box from which nothing could 5 escape, — the higher powers of energy tended always to fall lower, and that this process had no known limit.

The Second Law led to a preoccupation with the end of the world because it showed that the dissipation of energy was a one-way process and that, as a result, a time would come when 10 the earth was unfit for life.
And so it is that, as the Time Traveler drives on into the future, peculiar changes come over the earth. Day and night become longer, the sun moves more and more slowly across the sky. The great sun itself is changing, passing through an evolution in 15 which its color becomes redder as it cools, while the moon has disappeared. At one point the Time Traveler stops his machine to look at our dying world — "the picture of this lethargic dying world," wrote Norman Nicholson [in his book *H. G. Wells*, Denver, 1950, p. 28], "is among the most significant passages in the 20 popular literature of the last sixty years."

From *The Future as Nightmare. H.G. Wells and the Anti-utopians*, by Mark R. Hillegas, New York: Oxford University Press, 1967, pp. 32–33.

16. Visions of the End

Together with Utopias and cautionary tales, apocalyptic visions 25 form one of the three principal traditions of pre-20th-century futuristic fantasy. Visions inspired by the religious imagination go back into antiquity, but the influence of the scientific

1 **Helmholtz,** Hermann (1821–1894), worked in the fields of mathematics, physics, medicine, psychology and philosophy – 4 **granting that...** if it was supposed that – 5 **higher powers of energy** *here:* any object hotter than its surroundings and therefore acting as a source of heat – 8 **dissipation** loss, disappearance – 24 **cautionary tale** story, usually for children, containing advice or warning

imagination did not make itself felt in literature until the late 19th century, and the end-of-the-world theme maintained many of its religious overtones until very recently. The phrase itself has become rather loose in meaning — the idea of the end of 5 the world could be quite specific when the world itself was seen as essentially unchanging, governed solely by the divine will, but, once change became accepted and the Comte de Buffon's *Epochs of Nature* (1780) had popularized the notion that a whole series of "worlds" had occupied the Earth's surface, the finality 10 of any particular end of the world became dubious. A spectrum extends, therefore, from apocalyptic visions to disaster stories, and it is difficult to draw a dividing line; it would be over-pedantic to construe "world" as "planet".

The earliest scientific romances of world's end are the products 15 of Romanticism: De Grain ville's antiprogressive *The Last Man: or Omegarus and Syderia* (1806) and Mary Shelley's gloomy Great Plague story *The Last Man* (1826). Plagues were to remain one of the standard literary means of depopulating the world and destroying society, but a particular favourite of scientific 20 romancers is the cosmic disaster, introduced by Edgar Allan Poe in "The Conversation of Eiros and Charmion" (1839). All these are near-future stories, but as realization grew of the actual age of the Earth and the nature of the processes which changed it — popularized by Lyell's *Principles of Geology* (1830) — stories 25 based on a more acute scientific understanding began to appear. Two classics of this kind appeared within a year of one another: Camille Flammarion's *Omega* (trans. 1894) and H.G. Wells's *The Time Machine* (1895). [...]

Wells offered several versions of the end of the world, including 30 the cosmic disaster story "The Star" (1897) and the apocalyptic satire "A Vision of Judgment" (1899). For much of his life he believed that if a new world were to be built the old would have to be destroyed, and thus there is a persistent apocalyptic vein

7 **Comte de Buffon** (1707–1788), French naturalist – 9 **the finality of s.th.** the idea that s.th. is really the end – 13 **to construe** to understand, to interpret – 24 **Lyell,** Sir Charles (1797–1875), British geologist – 25 **acute** strict – 33 **vein** *here:* mood

in his writing. This is offset by the fact that whether he was writing grim stories of atomic war — *The World Set Free* (1914) — or satirical accounts of a new Noah — *All Aboard for Ararat* (1940) — he remained committed to the idea that Man must have a second chance. Only *The Time Machine* and the despairing *Mind at the End of its Tether* (1945) give way entirely to anxiety.

Wells's contemporaries were a little less fascinated by apocalyptic possibilities, but many indulged themselves at least once in the spectacular possibilities of doom. […]

The end of the world proved to have distinct limitations as a theme in popular literature. It had fine melodramatic qualities, but the conclusion in which the chosen few set out to begin a new world very quickly became a cliche. In order to infuse new dramatic potential there grew up a variant of the theme, in which the end of the world is foreseen and those armed with foresight set out to guard against eventualities (usually derided by their neighbours — but they laughed at Noah, too). […] It is amply represented in modern science fiction by stories in which only a few are able to escape atomic war in the shelters or escape into space when the sun goes nova. […] A rather more subtle version of this same variant explores the effect on various characters of the knowledge that the world will end. [A well-known example is Nevil Shute's *On the Beach* (1957)….]

It was in the 1930s that the idea emerged that we ourselves might destroy the world as weapons of war become more technologically advanced, an early novel advancing this notion being *Unthinkable* (1933) by Francis H. Sibson. The "ultimate deterrent" or "Doomsday weapon" was introduced (and quickly used) in *The Last Man* (1940) by Alfred Noyes. The anxiety reflected here was not unrealistic. […] After the War, of course, this species of apocalypse became dominant as the possibility

1 **to offset** to balance – 9 **to indulge o.s. in s.th.** to allow o.s. to do s.th. enjoyable –
21 **to go nova** (*of a star*) to become much brighter suddenly and then gradually
fainter – 29 **deterrent** a threat used to discourage the enemy – 29 **Doomsday** the last
day of the world's existence, when God will judge all people

of atomic holocaust lent a new pertinence to apocalyptic thinking. Suddenly it seemed entirely likely that the world would end with a bang and not a whimper after all. [...] A sign of the depth of the anxiety is the rapid proliferation of satires and black
5 comedies featuring apocalypses precipitated by carelessness, including [...] Kurt Vonnegut Jr.'s *Cat's Cradle* (1963) and *Dr. Strangelove* (1963) by Peter George. [...]

The same pattern of ironic despair, satire and grimly pessimistic "realism" extended into the 1960s and 70s, when
10 many more rationalizations for the sensation of imminent doom began to appear, including overpopulation and pollution. [...]

The cosmic vision story has become almost extinct in post-War science fiction as the terms in which we conceive of the end of the world have virtually reverted to those of 150 years
15 ago — it is once again a near future affair. The main difference is that in the past it was the divine will which would decide when and how the world would end, and God could always be relied on to pick the chosen few wisely. Now that Man is generally assumed to be in control of his own destiny it is much more
20 difficult to be confident of the calibre of the chosen, or even to be sure that anyone will survive. Though the Millenarian feeling which saturates modern science fiction is by no means new, the anxiety that goes with it has a new element within it. We are no longer optimistic regarding the salvation that we should like to
25 believe in.

From *The Encyclopedia of Science Fiction. An Illustrated A to Z*, ed. by Peter Nicholls, London: Granada Publishing Ltd, 1979, s.v. "The End of the World".

1 **to lend pertinence to** to make s.th. seem relevant or appropriate – 3 **whimper** gentle weeping - **with a bang and not a whimper** allusion to T. S. Eliot's lines "This is the way the world ends/Not with a bang but a whimper" (from "The Hollow Men") – 4 **proliferation** increase, spreading – 10 **rationalization** rational treatment, explanation – 10 **sensation** feeling – 13 **to conceive of** to think of, to imagine – 20 **calibre** quality of mind or character – 21 **Millenarian** *from:* millennium = a time of happiness and prosperity for everybody that will follow the Final Judgement or a catastrophe

The Film Version of *The Time Machine*

17. A Patronizing Simplification of the Story

TIME MACHINE, THE Film (1960). Galaxy Films/MGM.
Directed by George Pal, starring Rod Taylor, Alan Young, Yvette
5 Mimieux, Whit Bissel and Sebastian Cabot. Screenplay by David
Duncan, based on the story by H. G. Wells. 103 mins. Colour.
Unlike Pal's *War of the Worlds, TM* is set in the Victorian era at
the beginning of the film, and it is these sequences, with the
inventor demonstrating his creation to his disbelieving friends
10 amid the Victorian bric-a-brac of their cosy world, that work the
best. After a visually interesting journey through time (special
effects by Wah Chang and Gene Warren) the film reduces Wells's
angry parable to a Hollywood sf formula.

The symbolic parallels between the troglodyte Morlocks and
15 the Victorian working class, and the beautiful but thoughtless
Eloi and the Victorian upper class, are lost. The time traveller
becomes a confident, romantic hero, successfully rousing the
Eloi to battle against their apelike persecutors. The disturbing
evolutionary perspectives of the end of Wells's book are also
20 missing from the film. The work of the special effects men,
William Tuttle's make-up and the art direction of George W. Davis
and William Ferrari (whose design for the time machine is
charming) are all above average, but technical expertise does
not compensate for the patronizing simplification of the story.

25 From *The Encyclopedia of Science Fiction. An Illustrated A to Z*, ed. by Peter
Nicholls, London: Granada Publishing Ltd, 1979, s.v. "The Time Machine".

---

5 **screenplay** story written in a form suitable for its production as a film – 10 **bric-a-brac**
bits of old furniture, china, ornaments, etc. – 13 **sf formula** a set form or pattern of
science fiction – 14 **troglodyte** (*of prehistoric man*) living in caves – 18 **disturbing** *here:*
destroying one's peace of mind, causing anxiety

18. Expertly Crafted on All Counts

TIME MACHINE, THE
MGM (1960). Color, 103 mins.

In the year 1900, a young dandy named George (Rod Taylor)
5 experiments with time travel. Telling his skeptical friends Kemp
(Whit Bissell), Hillyer (Sebastian Cabot), and Philby (Alan Young)
that he will prove his time-traveling theory to be fact, he bids
them farewell. Good friend Philby sees something is amiss and
cautions George to be careful.

10 George pens a note to his old chum, instructing him to keep
an eye on his belongings when he is gone. He then enters his
basement workshop, climbs into a full-scale time machine, and
hurtles into the future.

He pauses during the World War I, when he finds London in
15 the midst of an air raid. He encounters Philby's son, who tells
him that his father took over George's home and refused to sell
it. In fact, it is still standing. George makes a stop or two more
before skidding to a halt in 1966, as an elderly Philby, Jr., herds
Londoners into an underground shelter at the beginning of
20 World War III. Atom bombs go off. Molten lava overtakes
London.

George dives into the machine and zips into the future, coming
to a halt in the postnuclear world of 802701. This world is
populated by the childlike Eloi, perennial teenagers who roam
25 the surface world, and the cannibalistic-mutant Morlocks, who
keep the Eloi fed and clothed before dragging them into the
underground to use them both as slaves and as food. Falling in
love with Eloi girl Weena (Yvette Mimieux), George decides to
help the Eloi fight the Morlocks. He leads them into the
30 underground tunnel armed with courage and 19th-century
firepower.

---

10 **to pen** to write (letter, etc.) – 10 **chum** *informal:* good friend – 13 **to hurtle** to rush
with great speed – 18 **to skid to a halt** to stop abruptly – 22 **to zip** *sl* to move at great
speed – 24 **perennial** remaining (teenagers) forever – 24 **to roam** to wander around –
25 **mutant** changed, having undergone a mutation

After defeating the Morlocks, he returns to the past to grab a few books and tools and rejoin his precious Weena. Only Philby believes what has happened, and he wonders aloud which books George brought into the future to rebuild the human race.

5   Expertly crafted on all counts.

From *The Science Fictionary: An A–Z Guide to the World of SF Authors, Films and TV Shows*, ed. by Ed Naha, New York: Seaview Books, 1980, s.v. "The Time Machine".